C000133004

DISCLAIMER

If You Read This LYBL Book You Are Liable To Live Your Best Life

Copyright © 2023 by Aiden Dogood
All rights reserved. No part of this publication may be reproduced,
distributed, or transmitted in any form or by any means, including
photocopying, recording, or other electronic or mechanical methods,
without the prior written permission of the author, except in the case of
brief quotations embodied in critical reviews and certain other
noncommercial uses permitted by copyright law.
Published by Amazon/KDP
Printed by Amazon.com
For permissions, please contact: Aiden Dogood
Contact@LiveYourBestLife.com
Visit the author's website at:
www.LiveYourBestLife.com
Special thanks to all of the teachers we mention in this book and all
who currently teach similar information to the world.

TABLE OF CONTENTS

INTRODUCTION

This is the ultimate guide for self-transformation. Even for those who do not feel they need help. This book holds valuable insights for both those seeking self-development and those not seeking it. Our goal is to encompass all facets of self-transformation, weaving together teachings from various self-help mentors and coaches. Recognizing that certain elements are sometimes overlooked in self-help, we have committed to bridging those gaps.

This book is also for people of all religions and beliefs or lack thereof. We understand that certain words and phrases can be intimidating, possibly leading to the dismissal of valuable information as "spiritual mumbo jumbo." We respect diverse perspectives, including those rooted in science and logic. We aim to provide a rational and accessible exploration of spiritual transformations without imposing specific beliefs. Regardless of your religious or spiritual background, we would like you to approach this book with an open mind. We're not asking you to abandon your beliefs; we want to help you understand your convictions.

Our team comprises individuals who have individually navigated the journey of personal transformation. Through our collective experiences, we have decided to share our insights and lessons in this book. Our approach begins with the understanding that personal change is the catalyst for success and happiness. Before achieving external success, one must cultivate an internal transformation. This is the fundamental principle we will impart throughout the book.

Consider this book as a step-by-step guide to becoming your best self. We'll present each concept methodically, allowing you to establish a solid foundation before moving to new insights. Specific *points may be repeated; this is intentional, as these are the cornerstone ideas crucial to your understanding. By the book's conclusion, we aspire to construct a comprehensive framework for you to live your best life.*

We intend to demystify the mystical and ensure that your pursuit of personal growth feels grounded and achievable. The destination we envision is not a far-fetched dream but a tangible kingdom of possibilities where our greatest aspirations reside. Though it may seem challenging, we assure you that the journey is undoubtedly worthwhile. Keep walking the path, and you will reach the kingdom of your brightest dreams—a realm where everything becomes possible within you.

Authors often invite readers into their personal worlds and backgrounds in traditional introductions. Each of us authors has faced unique challenges on the journey to becoming our best selves. Some grappled with profound depression, and others wrestled with persistent anxiety. Narcissistic tendencies and the loss of one's sense of self plagued some, while others battled pervasive self-doubt and a lack of hope. Each of us has overcome both mental and physical health problems in our journey, and we're here to teach you how to accomplish the same. Overcoming these hurdles varied in speed and process for each of us. Each of us embarked on an individual journey, ultimately reaching our desired destination by refusing to surrender to self-sabotage and hindering personal growth.

Echoing Woody Allen's wisdom that "80% of success is showing up," our collective experience underscores the importance of perseverance. By consistently showing up for ourselves, doing the necessary work, and persisting on the path, success becomes an inevitable outcome. Anticipating challenges and obstacles along the way is a reality we accept. The perspective we choose—whether viewing obstacles as opportunities for growth and learning or insurmountable barriers—shapes our journey.

Adopting a mindset that sees beyond problems and seeks solutions is crucial. Constantly dwelling on the difficulties, uttering phrases like "It's too hard," "I can't do that," or "I don't see how it's possible" acts as a roadblock to solving problems. The key is to look beyond the problem, shift our thinking, and actively seek solutions. We encourage you to maintain an open mind and cultivate positive thinking as you embark on this journey toward living your best life with us. Negative thinking, if unchecked, closes doors to the future you aspire to and veers you away from the path leading to the kingdom you seek.

"Living your best life" is a concept that embodies the pursuit of personal happiness, fulfillment, and self-realization. It involves aligning your actions, choices, and values with your authentic self, leading to a life that reflects your true desires and purpose. Living your best life is a dynamic and evolving process that requires self-awareness, intentionality, and a commitment to continuous growth. The importance of unleashing complete potential lies in its profound impact on an individual's well-being, success, and overall life satisfaction. When you unleash your full potential, you tap into your unique strengths, talents, and capabilities, allowing you to:

Achieve Fulfillment:
- Unleashing your full potential enables you to pursue activities and goals that resonate with your passions and values, bringing a deep sense of fulfillment and purpose to your life.

Maximize Productivity:
- By recognizing and utilizing your strengths, you can optimize your productivity and efficiency in various aspects of life, whether in your career, relationships, or personal development.

Experience Personal Growth:
- Unleashing your full potential often involves stepping out of your comfort zone, facing challenges, and embracing growth opportunities. This continuous process of self-improvement leads to a more resilient, adaptable, and evolved version of yourself.

Enhance Well-being:
- Living up to your potential improves mental, emotional, and physical well-being. It involves caring for your health, managing stress, and cultivating positive habits to support a balanced and harmonious life.

Build Meaningful Relationships:
- Authenticity and self-awareness are essential in building genuine connections with others. Unleashing your full potential allows you to engage authentically, fostering meaningful and supportive relationships.

Create a Positive Impact:
- When you leverage your unique skills and abilities, you can contribute positively to your community and the world. Unleashing your potential often involves sharing your gifts and making a difference in the lives of others.

In essence, unleashing your full potential is about living a purpose-driven life, realizing your capabilities, and embracing the journey of self-discovery and continuous improvement. It's a commitment to living authentically and intentionally, resulting in a rich life of meaning, joy, and fulfillment.

Within the pages of this book, we will delve into many topics, exploring what we term the 4 Ms: Matter, Meditation, Mindfulness, and Manifestation. Complementing these, we introduce the 4 Ps: Passion, Positive energy, Presence, and Personal reality. These principles intricately interweave to form the comprehensive framework we present. Our approach begins with establishing a foundational understanding and systematically building upon it, addressing each element piece by piece.

Embarking on this journey, we will begin by explaining the concept of energy and its pervasive influence on our world. The exploration extends to the laws of the universe, familiarizing you with their impact on our daily lives. Initiating the metamorphosis process, we will tackle prevalent issues and guide you toward steering your life in a positive direction. Self-awareness is pivotal in identifying your unique challenges, habits, feelings, and thoughts. Once these patterns and programs are recognized, we guide you in breaking detrimental habits and rewiring the programs shaping your existence.

Also central to this transformation is exploring forgiveness and facing fears—cornerstones in pursuing happiness. While not overly complex, this process demands effort, work, and a willingness to endure discomfort. The payoff, however, is the profound transformation from the old you to the best version of yourself. Throughout the journey, we provide tools, tricks, and tips to facilitate a smoother, more attainable change process. By the book's conclusion, we believe you will possess the tools to initiate personal change and embark on the path to living your best life.

Our dream, born from aspirations so expansive that they encompass the dreams of others, is the driving force behind this book. Shifting our focus from personal dreams to collective dreams for the world unlocked extraordinary possibilities in our consciousness. This book manifests that dream as a vehicle to awaken the world to what may have been overlooked due to societal limitations and closed-mindedness.

While we won't delve deeply into these societal intricacies here, our primary goal is to help you achieve your dreams without drastically changing your beliefs, including religious ones. The terminology we use to describe our beliefs is inconsequential; what matters most is how we live and comprehend the world. Expanding our knowledge, perspective, and mindset is the key.

We express our deepest gratitude for taking the initial step towards change—being open to transformation. Thank you for obtaining and delving into this book; we trust that clarity will follow your reading. Armed with newfound understanding, you will confidently stride onto the path ahead. We wish you to traverse the river of change without trepidation, embracing the growth that necessitates repeatedly returning to its waters. There is always room for further growth, another level to ascend. Rather than fearing the river, let's cross it together, one step at a time. As a collective, we believe everyone can achieve their goals and dreams. The pivotal question is: Are you ready to change? That is all that truly matters. Let's embark on this transformative journey together!

CHAPTER 1: THE FOUNDATION

We want to build a foundation before getting into the self-transformation guide. Understanding this foundation will help you with your transformation. We want to begin with what science has discovered about the universe thus far and unravel the profound connection between quantum physics, faith, religion, and spirituality, making it accessible to all, regardless of our beliefs. In our everyday lives, we navigate the world using our senses—seeing, hearing, touching, tasting, and smelling. This process is perception, the way we become aware of our surroundings. But there's more to our experience than meets the eye. Beyond perception lies perspective, our unique way of seeing and understanding the world. Shaped by personal experiences, beliefs, and values, our perspective is subjective and individual, creating a lens through which we interpret life's events. When we change our mindset, it then changes our perception of our reality. This is called a paradigm shift. A paradigm shift refers to a fundamental change in the basic concepts and practices of a particular idea, field, or belief system. It significantly transforms how people perceive, understand, or approach a specific subject. Paradigm shifts often lead to new perspectives, methodologies, or technologies, challenging established norms and leading to a different way of thinking or doing things. These shifts are crucial in driving innovation, progress, and evolution in various human knowledge and society areas. We plan for you to have many paradigm shifts while reading this book. Each new perspective builds upon itself to help you better understand life and how you begin changing yours.

Now, let's dive into quantum physics, a scientific frontier that might seem complex but is critical to understanding our existence. Planck, Einstein, and Bohr led the way in quantum physics. Quantum physics tells us that we are composed of 99.9999% energy and only 0.0001% physical matter. Each atom within us is 99.9999% energy, and only the protons, neutrons, and electrons comprise the physical matter of this atom. This tiny fraction of matter forms the basis of our physical bodies, while the vast majority is pure energy. This revelation leads us to a profound understanding: We are, at our core, beings of energy. Please think of this energy as the essence of our soul, the intangible force that defines who we are beyond our physical form. And the remarkable aspect? Energy cannot be created nor destroyed, echoing the age-old wisdom that the soul endures beyond our physical existence. Even atheists can get behind this concept.

If energy can only be transferred or transformed, then where does our energy go when we pass on? That's for another book in the future, but honestly, that answer doesn't matter for our current life. If we go into the ground as dirt, we should live our best lives while we're here because we don't get another chance. If we live another life after this one, we should still live our best life during this lifetime, too. And if we go to heaven or hell and never get another life, then we for sure need to live our best life during this lifetime...or else! No matter how you understand and interpret life, living well and prospering for the rest of this lifetime is our best interest.

Imagine the universe as an immense symphony and universal consciousness as the conductor that allows us to experience every note. In this state, we recognize that we are all connected by the same energy, fostering a sense of love and interconnectedness. Why are we here? Picture yourself as a lens through which consciousness explores and experiences different facets of existence. We become integral parts of a grander picture, with the source—call it God, the universe, or a higher power—acting as the artist orchestrating it all.

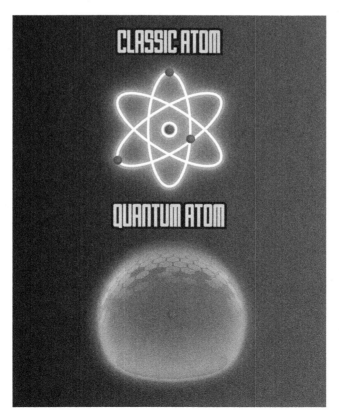

Enter the quantum field, a realm abundant with possibilities. Connecting with this energy brings forth a sense of unity and coherence, allowing us to experience love profoundly. The previous page presents a classic atom as we all perceive it and what an atom indeed looks like. The quantum atom better represents how we comprise 99.9999% energy and only 0.0001% matter. Knowing that we are energy, we expand to perceive a broader reality as we tap into these higher possibilities. Our thoughts influence our energy in our everyday lives, bound by time and space. Focusing on the past and our problems makes us feel disconnected, unaware that we are part of something more significant. When we explore higher possibilities, we start to experience a bigger reality. It's like playing a game where we can have different experiences on different levels. Right now, what we're going through is just one part of a much more extensive experience. In our everyday world, time and space limit us. Our thoughts influence our feelings, making us sometimes cut off from something more significant. If we keep thinking about things from the past, we might miss out on seeing ourselves as part of something much more important. Knowing that we are energy and part of something bigger means that what we think about shapes our reality. It's like the mind and the universe are connected. Everything is connected, even if it seems separate sometimes. Again, this information about being energetic beings does not need to shift your own personal beliefs to transform your life, but it will help you become more aware of energy itself and the power it possesses.

Religions often portray God as a powerful ruler to be feared, but what if we envision God as a reflection of ourselves? As we understand it, all religions teach that God is within us instead of without. God isn't an outside idol we must worship and fear. This change in perception of God can get lost in translation over time or simply from reading religious texts and then perceiving God in this fearful and distant way as opposed to a loving and fully encompassed way. If we see God as a mirror or a reflection of ourselves, the source or the quantum energy field becomes a vast pool of continually expanding awareness. Our hearts and empathy serve as links to this source. If the word God makes you cringe, then understand it as the love within yourself that connects you to everything around you instead of what separates you from everything. Understanding this connection empowers us to be creators of our reality. By choosing kindness and learning, we contribute to expanding universal awareness.

It's essential to recognize that God isn't here to punish but to reflect what resides within us. Therefore, we do not need to fear God nor feel like God is an idol to worship. Instead, God is the greatness within us, the love within us, and the universal consciousness that we can tap into by clearing our mind enough to remove the veil of the physical world and begin seeing the world as energy. So choose to be a creator, embrace love and universal consciousness, and unlock the door to a more meaningful reality. Remember, how you engage with this bigger picture shapes your truth. It's important to know that God isn't trying to punish us. Instead, it's like a reflection showing what's deep inside us. When we understand this, we can take responsibility for creating our reality and see how we're a part of something much bigger. So, choose to be a creator, embrace love and this particular feeling, and you'll unlock the door to a more meaningful reality. If you remember nothing from this chapter, then at least take this quote with you as you continue to read and as you continue to experience life:

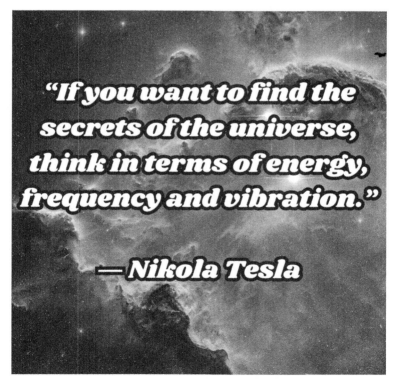

"If you want to find the secrets of the universe, think in terms of energy, frequency and vibration."

— Nikola Tesla

This is the perfect quote to help us shift our perspective. Albert Einstein also said, "Everything is Energy." If we can see and sense energy within and around us, we take a new approach to handling life instead of the physical matter approach we've used our entire lives. This understanding will help us lift the veil clouding our knowledge of life this whole time.

Since we are energy, we can learn to adjust our energy to experience life in the best way possible. We can control our energy, notice other energy around us, and keep other's energy separate from our own. We know we've mentioned quite a bit about God in this chapter, but moving forward, we will mostly stick to more of a scientific approach instead of using phrases such as God, soul, chakra, beliefs, etc. Quantum physics proves the existence of both souls and God, but there are other ways to explain them now than simply with religious faith. God can be described as the universal consciousness, the source, universal intelligence, etc. Souls can be described as conscious energy. Beliefs can be reframed as programs within ourselves, and chakras can be renamed as our energy centers. How do we know we are a soul and not just energy itself? Who observes our thoughts and feelings if we were just our physical mind and body? Who gets to decide the final verdict of each of our decisions? The voices we hear come from the mind, but who are these voices talking to? They're talking to us, the soul within this physical mind and body. That means we are the observer. We will use soul and observer synonymously throughout this book. We'll get more into these voices and how the mind, body, and soul connection work soon, but for now, we want you to know that we're not here to sell you on a specific religion, but we will explain energy, souls, and spirit and how they all affect our daily lives.

Your religious beliefs do not need to change in order to understand energy and how to transform your life. Having an open mind is essential for growth though. When we close our minds to only one perspective, one opinion, or one possibility then we limit growth within ourselves. Complacency and ignorance will keep us safe, comfortable, and secure, but these things will stunt our minds and our lives from progressing. Become your own duality, your own devils advocate, and your own therapist even. Think about the thoughts that come to your mind and question them. Do these thoughts come from source or do they come from ego? Is this an open-minded thought or a close-minded thought? What's another way to view this or another perspective to take? Does that new perspective align with you more than the first? Is there more truth in the second or third perspective than the first? Analyze yourself and find authenticity through analysis. The truth shall set you free, but it's going to upset you first. We may destroy our current bliss when we step out of ignorance, but we will find greater bliss in our new understandings.

As we venture deeper within ourselves, our spirit and soul are ever-present. If that sounds like crazy talk, please keep an open mind and give us a chance to explain. Even if you don't want to jump on the "soul train," you will still learn how to become your best self by the end of this book. So if the words soul, God, beliefs, chakra, etc. make you cringe, remember that you can replace those words with less cringey words within your mind. Please pay specific attention to the concepts if these words cause a negative response within you, and try to enjoy the lessons we have to teach you to help you live your best life.

CHAPTER 2: LAWS OF THE UNIVERSE

We want to continue to build upon the foundation by explaining many different laws of the universe. A quote from Aristotle sums this chapter up well. "We live in a world governed by law, not by change." This quote emphasizes the profound impact of universal laws on our lives, emphasizing that our existence is intricately bound by a set of principles rather than arbitrary happenstance. When applied to the laws of the universe, this perspective reveals our reality's structured and intentional nature. These laws shape our experiences and outcomes. Collectively, these laws create a framework that governs our lives' interplay of events and circumstances. They encourage us to understand that our destinies are not left to chance but are shaped by the deliberate interplay of these universal principles. Embracing and aligning ourselves with these laws offers a pathway to intentional living, helping us navigate challenges, make informed choices, and contribute positively to the interconnected tapestry of existence. In essence, recognizing and acknowledging the influence of these laws allows us to move beyond the realm of randomness, fostering a more profound sense of purpose and coherence in our journey through life. Let's get to know these laws of the univserse.

The Law of Cause and Effect:

- The Law of Cause and Effect is a fundamental concept stating that every event has a cause, and every cause produces an effect. This principle emphasizes the interconnectedness of events and rejects randomness. It operates in a temporal sequence, enabling predictability and forming the basis for scientific inquiry. The law extends to action and reaction, illustrating Newton's third law of motion. In philosophical contexts, it aligns with the concept of karma, linking actions to future outcomes. Ethically, it underscores personal responsibility, encouraging thoughtful consideration of consequences. The law highlights the interconnected nature of the universe and is integral to the scientific method, guiding researchers in understanding causal relationships. Embracing this law fosters a deeper comprehension of the consequences of actions and informs informed decision-making at both individual and global levels.

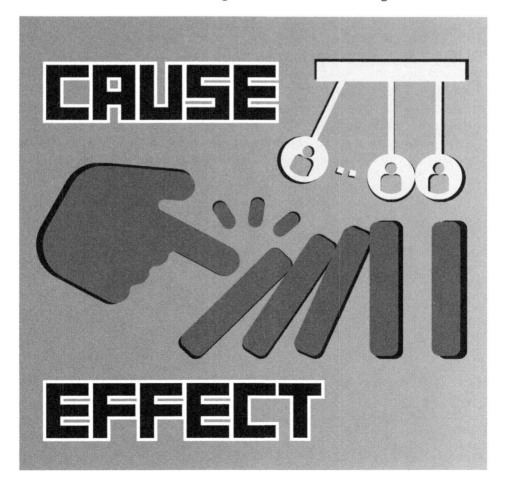

The Kybalion (a study of the hermetic philosophy of Ancient Egypt and Greece) teaches this profound principle: every cause yields an effect, and every effect has its cause. It dismisses chance as merely an unrecognized law. A simple example, like planting a tree years ago, resulting in its current growth, illustrates this principle. However, many life events are invisible, unlike visible trees or ripples in a lake. Consider someone who engages in workplace gossip, unaware that their casual words cause others to feel uncomfortable around them. They may wait to notice the growing distance or cold treatment from others. The effects of their gossip are consequences they unwittingly caused. Humans often focus on short-term thinking, but the Kybalion encourages understanding the significance of long-term effects. Pursuing dreams, for instance, may entail immediate sacrifices and hard work, but the enduring impact is a life of freedom and unique accomplishments. Similarly, embarking on a journey to improve physical health involves discomfort and sweat initially, yet the long-term benefits include confidence and overall well-being. Looking back at the decisions you made several months ago and how those decisions are now causing effects in your current life is a beautiful way to use this law to help yourself see how the things you cause end up having effects. It prompts reflection: "What results do I desire in my future, and what actions must I take today?" This approach invites you to consider the long-term consequences of your present choices, acknowledging that the beauty of life often unfolds gradually, shaped by intentional and mindful actions. So keep an eye on causes and effects within your own life and ensure you're causing the things you want to cause to gain the desired effects.

The Law of Correspondence:

- The Law of Correspondence, encapsulated by "As above, so below; as within, so without," reveals a fascinating connection between our lives and the patterns observed in nature. It suggests that the beauty and synchronicity we witness in the world around us are mirrored within ourselves. For instance, just as a solar system mimics the shape of an atom or a galaxy mirrors a hurricane, the principle proposes that natural patterns are reflected in our lives. By recognizing these patterns, we gain a powerful tool for personal growth. It encourages us to look inward, identifying moments when we were at our best and happiest, understanding that changing our inner world inevitably transforms our external reality. The Law of Correspondence invites us to find harmony within ourselves by recognizing the inherent patterns in nature and our lives.

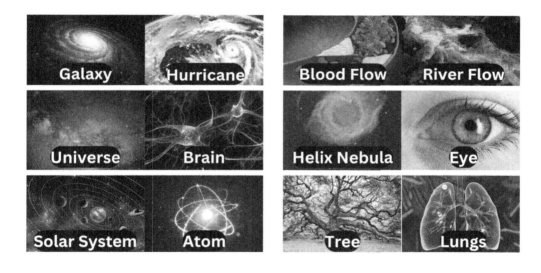

By recognizing these patterns in nature, we can recognize them within ourselves. If nature has patterns, it's likely our lives do too. Traditional self-improvement advice suggests modeling success after others who have accomplished what you would like to achieve. While it's wonderful to learn from others, a more assertive approach is modeling after yourself. We can take from the blueprints that others have laid before us and create our own blueprints in our own unique way. Besides simply looking at the patterns of others, we can also recognize the patterns in our own lives. And by changing our inner world positively, we can positively change our outer world.

Imagine the Law of Correspondence as a guide to finding your best self. It's a simple idea: what happens in nature mirrors your life. Picture the shape of a tree resembling your lungs or your eye resembling the pineal gland or helix nebulas. Nature's patterns are all around us. Now, think about your own patterns. When were you at your absolute best? Happiest? When did you feel like your best self? This law encourages you to look within yourself for inspiration rather than imitating others. Sure, other people are great, but modeling yourself is even better. Learn from others who have already done what you'd like to do with your life, but make it your own and add your own flare to everything. So, start with your inner world when you want to make positive changes. Reflect on the patterns that made you excel and be happy. By understanding and changing your inner world, you'll soon see your outer world looking pretty impressive. It's about discovering the patterns that make you shine and using them to become the best version of yourself. It all starts from within! If we wait for the outside world to change for us to change inside, then we may never change in the first place.

The Law of Attraction:

- The Law of Attraction is a metaphysical principle that suggests that like attracts like. In other words, the energy you emit through your thoughts, feelings, and actions will attract similar energies from the universe. This law is grounded in the belief that your thoughts can shape your reality, influencing the events, circumstances, and experiences that come into your life. Advocates of the Law of Attraction argue that maintaining positive thoughts and emotions can lead to positive outcomes, while negative thoughts may attract undesirable situations. The concept gained popularity through the New Thought movement and has been widely discussed in various spiritual, self-help, and personal development teachings. Here are the main principles of The Law of Attraction:

Like Attracts Like:

- This principle underscores the idea that the energy you emit into the universe attracts similar energy back to you. If your thoughts and emotions are positive, you will likely attract positive experiences and people into your life. Conversely, dwelling on negativity can draw more negative situations.

What You Think About, You Bring About:

- This principle emphasizes the power of thought in shaping your reality. The focus here is on the alignment of your thoughts with your desires. If you consistently concentrate on your goals and positive outcomes, you are more likely to manifest those desires.

Thoughts Are Things:

- This principle takes the concept further, suggesting that thoughts possess tangible energy with the potential to influence your reality. Your thoughts can impact your emotions, actions, and, ultimately, the events and circumstances that unfold in your life.

While these principles offer valuable insights into the Law of Attraction, it's essential to approach them with a balanced perspective. Rather than promoting a simplistic "don't think negative thoughts" mindset, it's crucial to recognize the complexity of human experiences. Some self-help teachers try to tell you that you should never think negative thoughts or else you'll manifest negative things into your reality. While there is some truth, it's often misleading and can lead to people ignoring and avoiding negative thoughts, which will not end well in the long run. We must embrace our negative thoughts enough to become aware of them, understand them enough to change, and forgive them so we can let them go. This is the only way to release our negative energy. Ignoring negative thoughts will only result in more frequent negative thoughts entering our minds. Eventually, they will become so strong that they can not be ignored anymore. Conversely, there is no need to constantly pay attention to and dwell on all of our negative thoughts. This, too, will lead to disaster and manifest negativity in our environment.

Here's a more nuanced approach:

Catch Your Thoughts:

- Instead of suppressing or avoiding negative thoughts, the emphasis is on awareness. Catching your thoughts involves mindful observation of your inner dialogue. Acknowledge negative thoughts without judgment, allowing yourself to understand their origin.

Change Your State:

- Once aware of negative thoughts, actively choose to shift your emotional state. This doesn't mean ignoring or suppressing emotions but engaging in activities uplifting your mood. Whether it's practicing gratitude, engaging in activities you love, or connecting with positive influences, consciously choose to change your emotional state.

Recognizing the potential harm in oversimplified advice that urges avoidance of negative thoughts or denies the importance of addressing past traumas is crucial. Exploring and understanding past experiences, learning from mistakes, and confronting unresolved issues are essential for personal growth. The Law of Attraction becomes a powerful tool when coupled with self-awareness, emotional intelligence, and a holistic approach to personal development. Embrace the positive energy of your thoughts while acknowledging and addressing the complexities of your past, allowing for genuine and sustainable transformation.

The Law of Inspired Action:

- The Law of Inspired Action asserts that meaningful progress and manifestation require more than thoughts and intentions—they demand purposeful and inspired steps toward your goals. It emphasizes that taking tangible actions aligned with your aspirations is crucial in realizing your dreams. It's a call to actively pursue your desires, understanding that intentional, inspired actions propel you closer to manifesting your visions.

Embrace the power of inspired action on your journey of manifestation. It's the transformative element often missing in the contemplation of our dreams. As John Maxwell wisely puts it, "Dreams don't work unless you do." Action holds a supremacy that surpasses mindset, beliefs, and thoughts. Consider this: one hour of purposeful action outweighs ten hours of meticulous planning. The question then becomes, "What can you do today?" It's a call to take a moment to take concrete steps toward your aspirations. The Law of Inspired Action reminds us that our dreams require contemplation and active participation. It urges us to be architects of our destiny, understanding that mere doing propels us closer to our goals than extensive planning periods ever could. So, in this moment, embrace inspired action. What step can you take today to breathe life into your dreams? It's not just about envisioning; it's about making those visions a reality through intentional, inspired action. Your journey awaits, and every step you take brings you closer to the manifestation of your aspirations.

The Law of Polarity:

- The Law of Polarity states that everything has an opposite or a polar counterpart. This law emphasizes that dualities, such as hot and cold, light and dark, or positive and negative, are inherent in nature. The understanding is that these opposites are not separate but are two extremes on the same spectrum. The law suggests that by recognizing and comprehending these polarities, we gain a deeper understanding of our lives full range of experiences and phenomena. This graphic below shows that everyone is on the same spectrum of narcissism and empathy or people-pleasing. It is often misunderstood that narcissists do not feel empathy. That description is for sociopathy, not narcissism. We all have some narcissistic tendencies as well as empathic tendencies. And we end up attracting the equal opposite partners to us naturally. The more extreme you are on this spectrum, the more toxic your relationships will be. The goal is to work towards the center of this spectrum, achieving a perfect balance of wholeness. In turn, you will attract a balanced, whole partner in life.

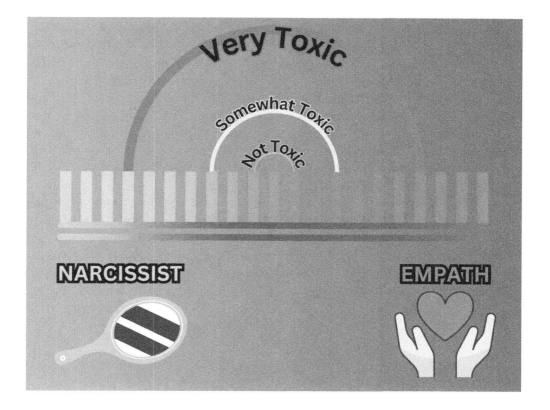

Embrace the profound wisdom of the Law of Polarity, for it unveils a universal truth that permeates every aspect of our lives. Recognizing that everything is dual, possessing poles and manifesting opposites, we uncover a rich tapestry of experiences shaping our existence. Consider the essence of this law: like and unlike are not separate entities but two sides of the same coin. Opposites, while distinct in degree, share an identical nature. It's a reminder that within every challenge lies an opportunity, within the darkness, a potential for light. Extremes, seemingly distant, converge, unveiling the interconnectedness of all things. In understanding the Law of Polarity, we appreciate the intricate dance between contrasting forces. It implies that our experiences of joy and sorrow, success and failure, love and loss are not isolated occurrences but interconnected elements of a broader human experience. "All truths are but half-truths," echoing through this law, invites us to explore the multifaceted nature of reality. It prompts us to question assumptions, seek the middle ground between opposing views, and recognize that our perspectives are inherently partial.

A helpful way to apply this to life is with relationships. Everyone is on the same spectrum of narcissistic and empathic. Interestingly enough, those closer to the extremes on both sides often experienced similar trauma in their childhood. They felt they could not be themselves without scrutiny or consequences, so they disowned part of themselves. Narcissists choose to create a fake persona to replace their self that isn't "good enough" for validation. Empaths decide to lose their self-identity almost completely and begin attaching to other people's energies, wants, and needs. This is why empaths are referred to as "people pleasers." They give up their wants and needs and seek validation by caring for others. Narcissists demand that others accept their fake persona and attend to their own needs. So essentially, it's a spectrum ranging from self-centered to selfless. On either side of the spectrum, fears, worries, and doubts push us away from the center where we feel whole as individuals. Are you more committed to living in fear than going all in? If you're holding things back, you will fear your partner is as well. Instead of looking for the right person, consider becoming the right person. Your relationships will only grow to the extent that you do. Become the change you want to see you in your relationships. It all starts with you. Change who you are within to see the changes in your life.

Selflessness is generally a positive quality to have. Still, when it becomes extreme, it can become a negative quality. This extreme is also commonly called "codependent," which means they depend on others for their validation, and they will attach themselves to more potent energy, no matter how toxic it is, to feel safe. We each tend to attract those on the opposite side of this spectrum. Extreme narcissists attract extreme empaths, moderate narcissists attract moderate empaths, and balanced individuals attract other balanced individuals. This explains the phrases "opposites attract" and "complete me." Most people believe it's "romantic" to look for a partner who will "complete" them. This is never a healthy relationship, though, and will surely end in disaster unless these two individuals somehow become whole around the same time as each other while in the relationship. This is highly unlikely but possible. A healthy relationship involves two complete individuals who do not "need" a partner but complement each other well and can harmonize. Two partners can grow together, learn from each other, and live more fulfilling lives by including each other in their goals and dreams. So, it is wise to understand where you are on this spectrum and recognize that you will attract the opposite type of partner. You will attract more wholesome partners as you grow and become a more wholesome person. The more extreme partners you used to attract and be attracted to will no longer suit you, and you won't feel connected to them like you used to.

This law also acknowledges the existence of paradoxes, those seemingly contradictory elements that challenge our understanding. Yet, it offers a profound promise — that all paradoxes may be reconciled. It's an invitation to embrace the complexity of life, knowing that within the apparent contradictions lie the keys to deeper understanding and personal growth. So, as you navigate life's dualities, remember that the Law of Polarity is not a force to resist but a guiding principle to embrace. Find solace in the understanding that every challenge carries the seed of opportunity; every setback holds the potential for a comeback. In the dance of opposites, discover the beauty of balance, and in embracing the complexity of paradoxes, uncover the richness of your own existence. This law is not a limitation but a gateway to profound wisdom, encouraging us to navigate life's spectrum with resilience, understanding, and an open heart.

The Law of Genders:

- The Law of Genders, a fundamental principle in Hermeticism, states that gender is inherent in everything. It goes beyond the traditional understanding of biological sexes and asserts that everything possesses masculine and feminine principles. These principles are not limited to physical aspects but also mental, emotional, and spiritual dimensions. The law emphasizes the interplay and balance of these gendered energies in the creation and manifestation of all things. In essence, the Law of Gender underscores the idea that a dynamic dance of complementary forces within every aspect of existence contributes to the continuous cycles of creation and transformation in the universe.

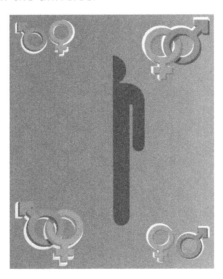

Embrace the Law of Gender, where masculine and feminine energies can work together. The Masculine urges disciplined goal-setting, conquering inner challenges, and constant focus. Meanwhile, the Feminine calls for present-moment authenticity, intuition, and emotional connection. These energies, often seen as opposing, coexist on the same spectrum, offering a holistic approach to life. Recognize that self-improvement and self-healing are intertwined forces. Balancing discipline with self-love allows for true accomplishment and fulfillment. It's an invitation to integrate both energies, creating a path that resonates with the symphony of your unique existence. Most of us have a stronger one out of these two energies and can use them as our strength to achieve goals, but it is wise to also work on and emphasize the weaker of our two energies to find a nice balance. Regardless of your gender, you'll achieve a more harmonious life if you can balance your masculine and feminine energies.

The Law of Vibration:

- The Law of Vibration states that everything in the universe is in constant motion and vibrates at a particular frequency. This includes thoughts, emotions, and matter. Each vibration emits energy and contributes to the overall energetic resonance of an individual or an object. The principle underscores that these vibrations are physical and extend to emotional and mental states, influencing the experiences and circumstances in one's life. Each musical note gives off a different vibration, and those vibrations form different patterns. Here's a picture of those patterns:

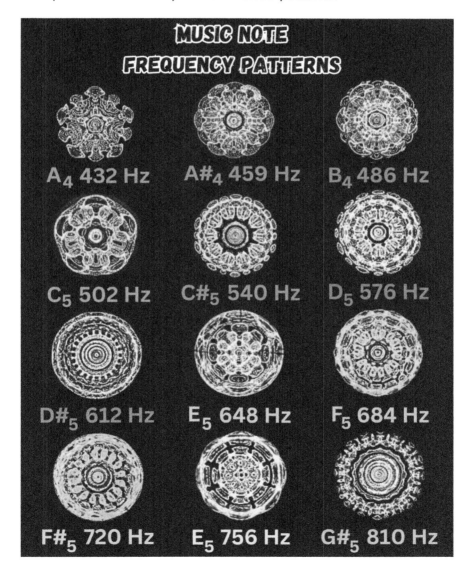

MUSIC NOTE FREQUENCY PATTERNS

A_4 432 Hz $A\#_4$ 459 Hz B_4 486 Hz

C_5 502 Hz $C\#_5$ 540 Hz D_5 576 Hz

$D\#_5$ 612 Hz E_5 648 Hz F_5 684 Hz

$F\#_5$ 720 Hz E_5 756 Hz $G\#_5$ 810 Hz

Isn't that visual representation of how sound waves beautiful? We sure think so! The Law of Vibration is a cosmic dance where everything is in motion, vibrating with energy and frequency. Once again, we return to Nikola Tesla's statement that understanding the universe means thinking about energy, frequency, and vibration. Here's the key: your emotions and feelings carry their own energy and frequency. They influence your personal vibration, your unique energetic signature. The power lies in your ability to consciously raise your vibe. Think of it as an inner journey. Identify what makes you feel positive and uplifted. Is it certain activities, people, or the content you consume? These are the keys to elevating your energy. You should focus on your own vibe, not trying to change others. You have the power to uplift your energy and attract positive experiences. Ask yourself: What brings me joy? Who inspires me? What content fuels my positivity? This self-discovery journey allows you to live with intention. You're the maestro of your own vibrational composition. You can choose the elements that resonate with your best self. Raising your vibe enhances your life and contributes to the universal symphony, creating a positive ripple in the cosmos. A beautiful side effect of raising your vibe is health. Our immune systems are directly tied to our emotions. The more often we feel great energetically, the more consistently our body will produce the right hormones, proteins, chemicals, etc., to aid us in functioning at our best and even reversing disease and sickness caused by repeated states of stress and low vibration. In later chapters, we will help you develop skills to keep yourself vibrating at a high frequency and give you external tools to help increase your own frequency.

The Law of Rhythm:

- The Law of Rhythm asserts that everything in the universe follows a natural flow and cycle. It emphasizes that rhythmic ups and downs, expansions, and contractions characterize life. This law underscores the inevitability of change and the importance of embracing the natural rhythms of life. The Law of Rhythm teaches us that life unfolds in a rhythmic pattern, much like the ebb and flow of the tides. It emphasizes that every aspect of existence, from emotions to experiences, follows a natural cycle of ups and downs, expansions, and contractions. This law invites us to recognize that change is inherent in life. In understanding and embracing the rhythmic nature of our journey, we gain insight into the cyclical patterns that shape our experiences. Just as the seasons change and the moon goes through phases, our lives follow a rhythm that brings challenges and opportunities.

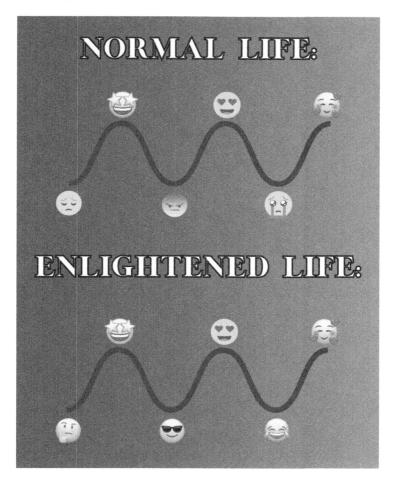

By aligning ourselves with the natural flow of these rhythms, we can navigate transitions with greater ease and resilience. Embracing the Law of Rhythm allows us to appreciate that, even in challenging moments, a positive shift is on the horizon, just as the sun rises after the darkest night. Ultimately, this law encourages us to go with the flow of life, recognizing that each phase serves a purpose in our personal and collective evolution. Understanding and harmonizing with the Law of Rhythm empowers us to live more authentically and gracefully through the various cycles of our existence. Instead of seeing certain moments as unfavorable, we can keep a positive mindset, knowing that this lesser moment will pass and a better moment is just around the corner. We can also appreciate the downs as lessons, obstacles, or challenges we need to face to grow. We can even elevate our energy by applying a mantra to each moment, such as, "This is exactly what I needed!" Even if you lose your phone or stub your toe, you can try to see it as something necessary for some reason. The reason will reveal itself if you keep paying attention and connecting the dots. Sometimes we won't see the dots connect, but just know that something as simple as losing your phone and arriving late to your destination may have saved you from a more significant tragedy like a car accident. This is the optimistic way of viewing life, and it's much more enjoyable than looking at life from a pessimistic perspective. Change your perspective, change your energy. Change your energy, change your life.

The Law of Compensation:

- The Law of Compensation explains that individuals receive a reward or retribution for their actions and efforts proportionate to the energy and intention invested. In simpler terms, it suggests that the universe compensates individuals based on the nature and extent of their contributions, whether positive or negative.

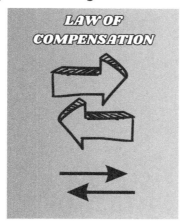

This law means to reap what you sow, a universal truth. "We get compensated as much as we give." -Ralph Waldo Emerson. This wisdom emphasizes that our rewards align with the effort and intention we invest. The principle is clear: "I'm someone who does the minimum" limits your rewards. Effort equals reward, a lesson known since childhood but often obscured by ego. This law invites us to break free from minimalism, recognizing that sincere dedication and genuine effort do not go unnoticed. Embrace the cosmic flow of compensation by infusing your actions with positivity, and witness a reality rich in fulfillment and abundant rewards. Your efforts will be noticed by the people around you and the universe itself. This even applies to yourself. If you know you did the minimum, you can't lie to yourself and act like you deserve a more significant outcome or reward for those minimal efforts. And when you give something your all, you will feel great about it regardless of the outcome. Feeling great about yourself is vital to living your best life. Even within relationships, give 100% instead of the bare minimum. We may be afraid to give something our all in fear that our greatest efforts won't be good enough. Where else in life are you not entirely all in? In what aspects do you have one foot in and one foot out just so if it doesn't work out, you can move on quickly and not be hurt by trying your best and failing? Failure is part of the process of success. So give your all and don't hold back; otherwise, you're setting yourself up for failure to begin with.

The Law of Mentalism:

- The Law of Mentalism asserts that "The All is Mind." It emphasizes the idea that the universe is fundamentally mental or consciousness-based. This law suggests that the mind is the foundational force shaping and influencing all aspects of reality.

The Law of Mentalism proclaims, "The All is Mind; the universe is mental." This principle unveils the power of thought control, meditation, and awareness to shape your emotional and physical states. In this journey of mental mastery, recognize that true strength lies not in reactive anger or impatience but in the calm resilience of a composed mind. Picture a serene lake undisturbed by ripples—a metaphor for the tranquil mind unswayed by minor disturbances. Mentalism invites you to transcend societal conditioning that links strength to reactivity, urging you to find true strength in thoughtful responses. Embrace this guiding light, cultivate mindfulness, and witness the profound impact on your well-being. In the realm of Mentalism, your mind actively shapes your reality. Let the serenity of a consciously composed mind inspire you to a life of profound influence and authentic strength. It all starts with your mind, so the more you become aware of how it works, the easier it will be to begin rewiring your mind and the habits you currently have. "We don't see things how they are; we see things how we are." -Joe Dispenza.

The Law of One:

- The Law of One is a spiritual principle emphasizing all things' interconnectedness. It states that every element of existence, from the smallest particle to the grandest cosmic entity, is interconnected and part of a unified whole. It underscores the idea that we are all intricately linked and that what affects one affects all.

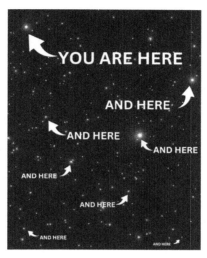

This spiritual principle whispers a universal truth—every atom, every being, every heartbeat is a note in the symphony of existence. In a world that sometimes seems fractured, the Law of One is a gentle reminder that we are not isolated entities but integral parts of a cosmic dance. It's an invitation to recognize the divine thread that weaves through the fabric of humanity, connecting us in a beautiful tapestry of shared experiences and emotions. As you navigate life, remember that your actions send ripples through this interconnected web. A kind word, a compassionate gesture— these small acts reverberate through the collective consciousness, creating a harmonious resonance.

So embrace the role you play. Your joys, sorrows, and aspirations are not solitary notes but harmonize with the universal melody. Let the Law of One inspire a sense of unity, empathy, and shared responsibility, for when we acknowledge the interconnectedness of all things, we step into a space where compassion becomes our guiding light. Allow this principle to infuse your interactions with kindness, understanding, and a profound awareness of our shared journey. In the Law of One, find the courage to be a beacon of light, illuminating the path for yourself and the entire cosmic symphony to which you are integral. "We are one!"

The Law of Relativity:

- The Law of Relativity is a principle that underscores the subjectivity of experiences and perceptions. It asserts that nothing in the universe is inherently good or bad; the meaning we assign to events and circumstances determines their significance. This law highlights the power of interpretation and response in shaping our understanding of the world. In this picture, we show how energy radiates from a central point and how it continuously flows. This picture is what is called a Torus Field. This is similar to the atom picture we showed before but shows more in-depth what a quantum atom looks like. All energy has a center/zero point and expands outwardly from that center point.

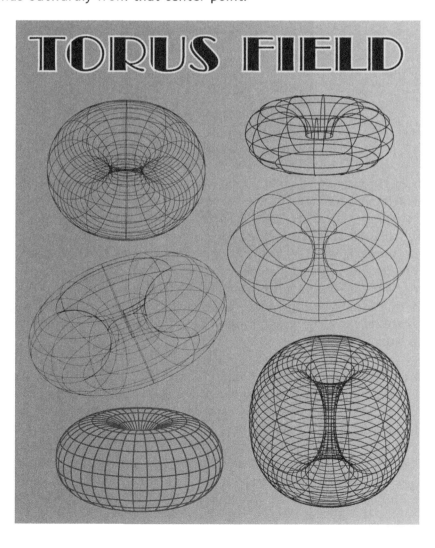

Within the Law of Relativity, the canvas of reality awaits the brushstrokes of your perspective. This cosmic principle whispers a timeless truth—nothing in the vast expanse of the universe carries an inherent label of good or bad. It is the lens through which we view the world that breathes life into our experiences. In this expansive universe of relativity, everything stands neutral, a blank slate eager for the colors of our interpretation. Your challenges, triumphs, and daily encounters lie in the realm of neutral potential, awaiting the artistry of your perception to define them. "Nothing is good or bad, but thinking makes it so." These words, echoing through the corridors of wisdom, invite you to recognize the extraordinary power you hold in shaping the narrative of your life. Every event, every encounter, every twist of fate is, at its core, neutral. It is your interpretation, your judgment, that breathes life into these moments.

While you may not control the events around you, the Law of Relativity places the extraordinary power of choosing how you respond in your hands. This choice becomes the alchemy that transforms the mundane into the extraordinary, the ordinary into the exceptional. Consider this profound truth: by altering the meaning you give to situations, you hold the key to changing your life. It's a realization that empowers you to shift perspectives, find hidden blessings in challenges, and uncover the silver lining in every cloud. Life has no meaning; we give it meaning by living it and perceiving it as we experience it. As you navigate life, remember that every moment is an opportunity to contribute to this majestic dance. No matter how small, your choices resonate with the universe's rhythm. Embrace the Law of Relativity, and let the awareness of this eternal dance inspire you to infuse every thought, every emotion, and every action with the transformative power that shapes the essence of your reality. Michael Singer sums up this law very well. He says, "Realize that it's not the moment in front of you that's bothering you. It's yourself bothering you about the moment in front of you."

Law of Perpetual Transmutation of Energy:

- The Law of Perpetual Transmutation of Energy is a fundamental principle that asserts the universe's constant energy transformation and flow. It states that energy is never stagnant; instead, it perpetually changes forms and moves from higher to lower vibrations. This law emphasizes the dynamic nature of energy and its responsiveness to our thoughts, emotions, and actions.

The Law of Perpetual Transmutation of Energy is where the very fabric of the universe is woven with threads of ceaseless transformation. This cosmic principle whispers a timeless truth—energy is the eternal dancer, forever pirouetting from one form to another. Imagine the vast symphony of existence, where energy takes center stage, moving in an ever-flowing choreography. Your thoughts, emotions, and actions, akin to the graceful strokes of a conductor's baton, influence this cosmic ballet. The energy around you is responsive, malleable, and in a perpetual state of transmutation.

In your life, recognize that you are the orchestrator, the maestro conducting the symphony of your own existence. Your thoughts hold the power to transmit energy from one state to another. Like an alchemist, you can transform the mundane into the extraordinary and the ordinary into the exceptional. Consider this profound truth: as you align your thoughts with higher vibrations, you become a channel for the perpetual transmutation of energy. Your positivity, kindness, and aspirations send ripples through the cosmic dance, elevating the vibrational frequency of the energy around you. As you navigate life, remember that every moment is an opportunity to contribute to this majestic dance. No matter how small, your choices resonate with the universe's rhythm. Embrace the Law of Perpetual Transmutation of Energy, and let the awareness of this eternal dance inspire you to infuse every thought, every emotion, and every action with the transformative power that shapes the essence of your reality. "Energy cannot be created or destroyed; it can only be changed from one form to another." -Albert Einstein.

The Law of Purpose (Dharma):

- The Law of Purpose, often called Dharma, is a guiding principle that emphasizes living in alignment with one's true nature and unique life path. It suggests that each individual has a distinct purpose or calling and encourages pursuing activities and choices that resonate with one's authentic self. Dharma underscores the idea that fulfilling one's purpose contributes to personal fulfillment and the greater harmony of the universe.

This timeless principle tells us that each person has a unique life purpose. In a world that often clamors with distractions and noise, the Law of Purpose invites you to attune your inner compass to the song that resonates deep within. Dharma suggests that you are not a mere wanderer but a purposeful seeker, navigating the seas of existence guided by the compass of your authentic self. Consider this: just as every note in a symphony contributes to the beauty of the composition, so does each individual's purpose add a unique richness to the grand tapestry of creation. Your purpose is not a destination but a journey, a continuous exploration of self-discovery and growth.

As you traverse life, the Law of Purpose encourages you to embrace your authentic essence, listen to your heart's whispers, and dance to the rhythm of your unique calling. Fulfilling your purpose is not a solitary endeavor but a harmonious collaboration with the universe, a dance where your steps synchronize with the cosmic choreography. In recognizing and living your purpose, you become a beacon of inspiration, radiating light for yourself and those around you. Your fulfillment echoes through the interconnected web of existence, contributing to universal harmony. Embrace the Law of Purpose, and let the awareness of your unique calling infuse every choice and action with intention. Your purpose is not a distant star but a guiding light within, illuminating the path to a life that resonates with authenticity, fulfillment, and a profound sense of connection to the greater cosmic purpose. So be your authentic self. If you don't know who your authentic self is, then it's time to start discovering that within yourself.

Now that we have introduced the laws of the universe, which are present everywhere, please keep these laws in mind as we progress through the book and as you progress through life. The patterns are endless, and being able to notice them can change the way we view our lives and the world around us. Changing how you view and see life dramatically changes how your life unfolds. This relates to your RAS (Reticular Activating System). If we told you to close your eyes and think of the color red, you would open your eyes and immediately be drawn to the red things around you. Our RAS can change instantly, just like in the example of thinking of the color red. When you start to pay attention and invite these laws of the universe into your RAS, life begins to have new meaning, and you start paying attention to broader things like the energy within everything and the energy all around you.

CHAPTER 3: YOUR PROBLEMS

Now, it's time to begin the transformation. We want you to learn how to become your best self and live your best life. This chapter isn't easy, but we know you're ready. Buckle up because here comes the bomb we must drop to start the changing process: ALL OF YOUR PROBLEMS HAVE YOU AT THE CENTER OF THEM.

Reading that last line may have triggered you. You may have felt a jolt of energy run through your body. And you may be hearing the voice in your head tell you that it was a ridiculous statement. "How can I be the problem? How am I at the center of each of my problems? That can't be true. My ego won't allow it to be true!" It's okay; take a deep breath and let those thoughts go. We'll explain this concept in more detail and more empathetically. So, how are you at the center of all of your problems? Well, let's recount the Law of Relativity, which once again is best summarized in Michael Singer's quote: "It's not the moment in front of you that's bothering you. It's yourself bothering you about the moment in front of you."

This statement may induce adverse reactions and turn on a light bulb for others. Michael is saying here that each moment in life isn't what's bothering us. We are allowing our ego and our negative experiences to attach a negative emotion to that moment, which in turn makes negative thoughts begin to narrate a story within our mind about that moment. The moment had no narrative until your mind reacted and gave it a narrative. Life is wholly comprised of non-emotional moments or neutral moments/events.

Even an event that most would categorize as "good," like a wedding, can be adverse if negative energy is present. Conversely, an event that most would classify as "bad," like a funeral, can be positive if there is enough positive energy within you and those around you. We, ourselves, attach an emotion to that moment to give it meaning. And this is how we remember things. Memories are thoughts and emotions about a particular moment or event. We burn that memory into our minds by attaching an emotion to an event. So, most mundane things are forgotten because we link no emotion to them. Therefore, they have no meaning to us, and the brain decides to move those mundane memories into the trash bin in order to make room for the things that matter and have meaning.

You've got to get past yourself. Become the observer of your thoughts, feelings, and actions instead of the reactor. Recognize that the moment in front of you is just a moment, and perhaps it's a necessary moment in your life to experience a more significant outcome down the road. Keeping the mantra, "This is exactly what I needed," in mind can help us find the positive within each moment, even when that positivity is more challenging to find. When you recognize your emotions, feelings, and thoughts, you can observe them and not let them become the narrative just because they're present. We think and feel many untrue things throughout the day, and it's up to us to decide which ones we pay attention to/give our energy to. "Where we place our attention is where we place our energy." -Joe Dispenza.

Eventually, you realize there's no real reason to be bothered and that any problem can be fixed by changing how you think and feel about it. This isn't delusional; it's just a way of looking at reality. There's the "glass half full" way of seeing things, and there's the "glass half empty" way of seeing things. We can change our perspective and/or mindset and find a positive way to observe the situation. This is what some people call looking for the silver lining. Looking for the silver lining in everything is akin to seeing the world through a positive lens. This much brighter lens allows more light to pass through it. Some people call this lens that helps us see the positive in everything "Rose-Tinted/Colored Lenses." If we want to call this perspective/mindset/lens the "rose-tinted lens," then we'd like to call the negative perspective/mindset/lens the "dark-tinted lens." We picture aviator sunglasses mainly because some people call them "assholes." And that term is perfect for this analogy because that's exactly how you act when you have dark-tinted aviators. When you see the world, life, and yourself in a negative light, you tend to act like an asshole to yourself and others. We can all agree that this is not the way we want to live, and it's not the way we want to see our reality. "You have within you right now everything you need to deal with whatever the world can throw at you," said Brian Tracy. Let's take a moment and define and discuss perspective, mindset, and the lens through which we see reality.

Perspective and mindset are related concepts that influence how individuals perceive and interpret the world. While they share similarities, there are nuanced differences between the two:

Perspective:
- **Definition:** Perspective refers to a particular way of viewing things, influenced by experiences, beliefs, values, and cultural background.
- **Nature:** It's a broader term encompassing overall outlook or worldview.
- **Flexibility:** Perspectives can be fluid and subject to change based on new experiences or information.
- **Example:** Someone may have a positive perspective on challenges, seeing them as opportunities for growth.

Mindset:
- **Definition:** Mindset is a set of attitudes, beliefs, or mental frameworks that shape how individuals approach situations and make sense of their experiences.
- **Nature:** It's more focused on cognitive patterns and habitual thinking.

- **Influence on Behavior:** Mindsets influence behavior and responses to challenges.
- **Example:** A growth mindset involves seeing abilities as malleable and can be developed through effort.

Relation to the Lens of Reality:

- Perspective can be seen as the broader lens through which individuals view the world. It includes their overarching worldview, shaped by personal experiences and cultural influences.

Mindset as a Cognitive Filter:

- Mindset, on the other hand, functions as a cognitive filter that influences how individuals interpret and respond to specific situations within their broader perspective.

Dynamic Interaction:

- Both perspective and mindset interact dynamically. A person's overall perspective might shape their general mindset, while specific mindsets can influence how they interpret individual events.

Impact on Reality Construction:

- Together, perspective and mindset play a crucial role in constructing an individual's reality. They shape perceptions, attitudes, and the meaning assigned to various experiences.

Application:

- Perspective in Relationships: In a relationship, an individual's perspective might involve their overall view on human connections, while their mindset could influence how they approach and navigate specific relationship challenges.

Mindset in Learning:

- In an educational context, a student's perspective might involve their general belief in the value of education, while their mindset would influence their approach to learning, such as having a growth mindset towards academic challenges.

Change and Growth: Changing Perspectives:

- Experiences and learning can lead to shifts in perspective over time, broadening one's overall outlook on life.

Developing Mindsets:

- Individuals can intentionally cultivate specific mindsets, such as a positive or growth mindset, to influence how they approach challenges and opportunities.

Conclusion:

- While perspective and mindset are distinct concepts, they are interconnected elements that collectively contribute to an individual's lens of reality. Perspective provides the overarching worldview, while mindset influences cognitive patterns and responses within that worldview. Both are dynamic and can evolve over time with conscious effort and experience. In essence, change the way you view things to change your life. We want to share some nuggets of wisdom that may help induce changes in perspective or a paradigm shift. So here is a list of beautiful quotes that may help you change your lens from dark aviators to rose-tint:

Here is a list of beautiful quotes that may help you change your lens from dark aviators to rose tint:

"We can't solve problems using the same kind of thinking we used when we created them." -Albert Einstein

"We don't HAVE to do anything; we GET to do anything." -Unknown

"Whoever fights monsters should see to it that in the process he does not become a monster." -Nietzche

"A change of feeling is a change of destiny." -Unknown

"You need power only when you want to do something harmful; otherwise, love is enough to get everything done." -Charlie Chaplin

"War does not determine who is right; only who is left." -Unknown

"The art of knowing is knowing what to ignore." -Rumi

"Focus on improving yourself, not proving yourself." -Unknown

"Love all, trust a few, do wrong to none." -William Shakespeare

"Apologizing does not always mean you're wrong and the other person is right; it just means you value your relationship more than your ego." -Unknown

"We are all one. Only egos, beliefs, and fears separate us." -Nikola Tesla

"A true leader doesn't create separation. A true leader brings people together." -Unknown

"The hardest part about change is not making the same choices we made the day before." -Joe Dispenza

"Doors are opening. The wait wasn't punishment; it was preparation." -Unknown

"Our eyes only see what our mind comprehends." -Robertson Davies

"Your triggers are your responsibility; it's not the world's obligation to tiptoe around you." -Unknown

"Do just once what others say you can't do, and you will never pay attention to their limitations again." -James R. Cook

"Old keys don't unlock new doors." -Unknown

"Life happens for us, not to us." -Tony Robbins

"Detachment does not mean you own nothing; it means nothing owns you." -Unknown

"To be able to shape your future, you have to be able to be willing and able to change your paradigm." -Joel Barker

"Your mind believes everything you tell it; give it love." -Unknown

"Mistakes are always forgivable if one dares to admit them." -Bruce Lee

"We wish that we could tell you it gets better; it doesn't; you get better." -Unknown

"We are only limited by weakness of attention and poverty of imagination." -Neville

"Make your vision so clear that your fear becomes irrelevant." -Unknown

"We don't see the world as it is; we see it how we are." -Joe Dispenza

"Don't adapt to the energy in the room; influence the energy in the room."
-Unknown

"Your life becomes a masterpiece when you learn to master peace."
-Unknown

"Be grateful for your triggers; they point you to where you are not free."
- Elizabeth McWilliams

CHAPTER 4: FIND YOUR PASSION

To begin this path of self-transformation beyond learning to see or view life, we must also establish a path for ourselves. Connect to our intuition and our passions in life. What excites us? What makes us feel joy and excitement? These questions help us define our path, which we will expand upon in this chapter. Many of us may struggle to find our calling, path, dream life, etc. So we'd like to help you find that thing that makes you feel fulfilled. You can start by thinking about what you're already good at. What are your talents? We're not sure what you consider yourself currently good at, but your passion isn't always necessarily something you're already good at. Also, understand that you can have many passions that make up your dream life and fulfill your calling or destiny. Your best self doesn't have to be limited to being great at just one thing. Let's say you're a hairstylist, and you like it, but it still feels like work to you. Your day is filled with ups and downs, primarily based on your fellow hairstylists' and customers' moods. Sometimes, your mood was already set from your time at home before work, or you allowed traffic to upset you. We're sure you've heard from your boss(es) that you must leave your problems and drama at home (which would be wise). That's a mindfulness technique that most already practice in our lives. Anytime you've calmed yourself down to help yourself be more successful with whatever you're about to do, you're practicing mindfulness. We'll also teach you how to stay aware of when this happens and how to become more effective at this mindfulness technique later in the book. Back to the hairstylist example for now, though. You like the work, but it still feels like work, and you've heard before that when you do something you love, it doesn't feel like work. We find that statement paramount in the discussion of finding your passion. So you like helping people and feel you get to help your customers by having a great haircut or style, but it just doesn't resonate in your heart. You don't feel like this is what you were put here to do. So, how do you discover what you were meant for? We do want to reiterate that this is just an example. Many people find passion in styling hair; there is nothing wrong with that. The point is that if you're not currently pursuing your passion, you're pursuing someone else's passion for them. "Your time is limited; don't waste it living someone else's life." -Steve Jobs.

Well, let's start deep-diving into things you enjoy doing. Hobby-wise, experience-wise, fun-wise, etc. What puts a smile on your face? What could you do to help the world become a better place? Or at least what could you do to make you feel like you positively impact the lives of those you encounter? Maybe think of this: "What could I teach someone right now that would make me feel joy for teaching others?" We believe that one of the main reasons for life itself is to create. That's reproduction and evolution at its finest. Through reproduction, we hope to create a new life in this world and make that new life better than our own. Being a creator of something is not only a very spiritual act, but it tends to be one of the most lucrative things you can do. Art is subjective, meaning whatever you make will be priceless to some; to others, it won't mean anything to them. This doesn't mean everyone's calling is to become an artist. There are many less artistic forms of creation, so please don't think we're just telling you to quit your day job and pick up a paintbrush or a guitar. But we're also not telling you not to do that. So, let's continue exploring what else may help you find your passion(s).

Don't just limit yourself to what you've experienced or what you're already skilled at. Think of other people you've met who found their passion and how you wished you were doing what they were doing. If you discover something you feel at home with but don't know much about how to do it, don't fret. Learning most skills doesn't have to take long or large sums of money. Especially computer-related skills like making videos, designing music, voice recording, writing stories, poems, etc. Creative things that come from your heart can be monetized and can be taught. You can also bring creativity into other businesses that aren't considered artistic. You can think outside the box and develop new strategies, concepts, or ideas for whichever business you find your passion within.

Search your mind for the things that bring a smile to your face. And think of how you want to make your mark on this world. What do you want to be remembered for? You know what that thing is most likely, and you may have buried it inside yourself due to a fear of failure. Remember that no matter what you do, in the beginning, you will be horrible at it. No matter how much you study it first, trying it out will be challenging, and you will be bad at it compared to others who have been doing it for much longer and even compared to yourself later down the road when you have been doing it much longer, so don't let that stop you in your tracks. Compare your today self with your yesterday self if you're going to make any comparisons. There is no need to include others or your potential future self in your comparisons. It will only make you feel inadequate if you obsess over comparing yourself to others. If none of this advice seems to help you find your passion, then perhaps asking yourself your core values could help. If you have clear values, this may help you at least narrow your vision towards a few things that may be your passion. You could also try tools like StrengthsFinder or VIA Character Strengths to identify natural talents and strengths. If none of this seems to be helping, then you may just not be ready to find your passion. You may need to wait until you've become more of your best self to find that passion. Here are some questionnaires that may help you discover your passion:

Quick Guide For Finding Your Passions:

1. Write down everything that excites you and you enjoy doing, including things you used to do in your past that you don't do anymore.

2. Write down your current skills and talents.

3. Cross out all things previously written that seem difficult or impossible to make money doing.

4. Circle the best things you believe would benefit the world and possibly help others.

Whatever you end up circling is a possible passion of yours. Take this list of circled items and choose which ones you'd like to pursue today.

Extensive Guide For Finding Your Passions:

Section 1: Reflection on Passions

1. What activities or hobbies make you lose track of time when you're engaged in them?

2. Think about moments when you felt truly alive and fulfilled. What were you doing, and why did it make you feel that way?

3. Consider the subjects or topics you naturally gravitate towards. What knowledge or skills do you enjoy acquiring?

Section 2: Identifying Strengths and Talents

4. List three skills or talents you feel confident about.

5. Reflect on compliments you've received from others. What do people often acknowledge you for?

6. What would you choose if you had to teach someone a skill? Why?

Section 3: Values and Beliefs

7. Identify three values or principles that are most important to you.

8. Consider causes or issues that resonate with you. What societal problems or challenges do you feel passionate about addressing?

9. Imagine a world where you've made a significant positive impact. What kind of change have you contributed to?

Section 4: Dreams and Aspirations

10. Envision your ideal life ten years from now. What does it look like? Include aspects such as career, relationships, and personal development.

11. What project or endeavor would you pursue if you had all the needed resources?

12. What legacy do you want to leave behind? How do you want to be remembered by others?

Section 5: Overcoming Obstacles

13. Reflect on past challenges you've overcome. What strengths or lessons did you discover about yourself through those experiences?

14. Identify any fears or doubts holding you back from pursuing your dreams. How can you address or overcome them?

15. What bold steps would you take toward your calling or dreams if failure was not an option?

Conclusion: Action Steps

16. Based on your responses, what are three actionable steps you can take in the next month to explore and pursue your calling or dreams?

Remember, this questionnaire is a tool for self-reflection, and there are no right or wrong answers. Encourage yourself to revisit your responses periodically as your insights may evolve.

We believe the most significant question to ask yourself is: **"How can I spread my love to the world in the best manner?"** And it doesn't have to be one way, business, or medium. Find the love inside you and ask yourself how you can best express it to the world.

No matter what you do end up discovering to be your calling or passion, it's not the ONLY thing or things you were meant to do. You were meant to create wonderful relationships with people, build great memories, and have beautiful experiences. People are remembered for what they did for the world and created, but more so than that, they are remembered through their experiences with others. Even some of the greatest business people's funerals are full of stories about what they did for those in their lives and how that person brought joy to the people they left behind. Not as much is generally shared about the work they left behind. The most common regrets people have on their deathbed are about not pursuing their dreams. Not trying harder and not giving their dreams a chance. So focus on figuring out how to become the kind of person who tackles each moment with love and brightens people's days with your words and the energy you spread to them. The rest will work itself out. Become the change you want to see in the world, and your energy will shine bright enough to have your many different dreams pulled toward you. Just keep smiling and keep loving yourself and other people. A good mental exercise to help you become more joyful is asking yourself some questions. How can you make each moment better than when it presented itself to you? How can you take a simple situation and make it an elevated experience? How can you transform someone's negative energy into positive energy? How can you seize the day and feel like you lived your best day? Find that day in your mind and what it consisted of, then do it today. And then do it tomorrow and the next day and grow each time. Then, reflect on your day before bed, think about how you could have done better, and mentally rehearse what you will do next time instead. There's no need to beat yourself up for not doing your best; just keep it in mind and rehearse a better approach for next time.

Here are the 5 Big Personality Traits that may help you narrow down who your best self is as well:

PERSONALITY TRAITS

	CONSCIENTIOUSNESS	
IMPULSIVE		CAREFUL
DISORGANIZED		DISCIPLINED
	AGREEABLENESS	
SUSPICIOUS		TRUSTING
UNCOOPERATIVE		HELPFUL
	NEUROTICISM	
ANXIOUS		CALM
PESSIMISTIC		CONFIDENT
	OPENESS TO EXPERIENCE	
ROUTINE		SPONTANEOUS
PRACTICAL		IMAGINATIVE
	EXTRAVERSION	
RESRVED		SOCIABLE
THOUGHTFUL		FUN-LOVING

"The only person you are destined to become is the person you decide to be." -Ralph Waldo Emerson. Become that person you want to be now. Hold yourself to that standard. Walk in the shoes of your best self. And understand that you'll make mistakes and not fully be that person at first, but your accountability will fix those mistakes. We don't have to be upset at ourselves for failing to be the perfect person we want to be. Mistakes are just more info for us on how to get something right the next time or at least do better at that thing next time. So feel your best self and encourage yourself to improve with positive reinforcement. No need to look back with pain and regret. Look back to see all the progress you've made, all the things you've learned, and all the changes you've made along the way. Change is the natural course of life, so there's no need to fear it. Without change, there is no growth. Don't forget that you can't find your dreams if you continue to be the same person. Your old self has to die in the process so that you can break out of that cocoon and fly straight towards those dreams. You'll never get there as a caterpillar. You must become the butterfly. Your wings aren't going to work well at first, but don't let that make you decide to curl back up into your cocoon. Keep flying no matter what gets in the way, how much your wings tire, and how hard the wind blows. Just keep flying!

CHAPTER 5: MIND BODY AND MORE

To begin understanding how to change our perspective or the lens which we view reality through, we want to explain how we picture the relationship between our mind and body as well as where we (ourselves) fit into the picture and what the different voices we tend to hear within our minds as well. We have a chart so everyone can relate regardless of their religious beliefs. We use the word observer, synonymous with soul, and guide, synonymous with spirit. We are each the observer, and our spirit/guide/higher self is one of the voices we hear in our mind, even though it doesn't necessarily live in our mind. Our guide is what links us to the source/universal consciousness/God.

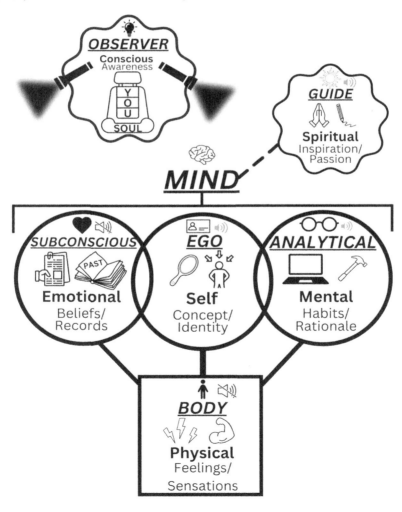

In these figures, you can see that we are seated within consciousness. We will use the words from this chart as we explain, so replace observer with soul and guide with spirit as you read this chapter if you are spiritual/religious. We used a car seat because we, as the observers, are the drivers of the consciousness. Without us (the observer), there is no consciousness. This is separate from the conscious mind. The conscious mind refers to whatever our consciousness is aware of within our mind. So consciousness is our awareness of anything, and our conscious mind is whatever we are aware of and paying attention to within our mind. We separate consciousness from the mind because we know we can be conscious of other things besides our mind and body. This is why we didn't draw a line from consciousness to anything else because we can become conscious of different parts of our mind, different parts of our body, and things outside of our mind and body. Picture consciousness as a cloud that floats around and shines a light on the rest of this diagram and everything in our surroundings. We can be conscious of the world around us and even more extensive dimensions than the 3D world that our mind and body live in. We call the quantum dimension 5D. 4D is the void that separates the 3D and the 4D. 4D is expressed as nothingness or as time itself. Time is what separates the 3D from the 5D. We don't want to lose you quite yet with the spiritual speak of other dimensions and spiritual lingo that may seem like fantasy as opposed to reality. So, let's stay in reality for now and talk about the rest of the diagram in this figure. Below the consciousness, we show how the mind operates. The analytical mind, the subconscious, and the ego.

The analytical mind is the cognitive capacity for critical thinking, logical reasoning, and problem-solving. It involves analyzing information, making decisions, and systematically processing data. Its function is crucial for evaluating situations, solving complex problems, and making rational decisions based on available information. Next, we have the subconscious mind.

The subconscious mind operates below the level of conscious awareness and contains information, memories, beliefs, and automatic responses that influence behavior. It shapes behavior, emotions, and perceptions based on past experiences and conditioning. Last, in the mind, we have the ego.

The ego is a psychological construct representing an individual's sense of self, self-identity, and self-awareness. It encompasses conscious thoughts, beliefs, and perceptions about oneself. It mediates between the demands of reality, the id (basic instincts), and the superego (moral values). It plays a role in decision-making, self-esteem, and identity or self-concept formation.

Now let's explain how these three parts of the mind work together:

Relationships Between The Analytical Mind, Subconscious, And Ego:

Integration of Conscious and Subconscious:
- The ego serves as a bridge between the conscious analytical mind and the subconscious. It integrates conscious thought processes with deep-seated beliefs and automatic responses stored in the subconscious.

Influence on Decision-Making:
- The analytical mind, driven by logic and reasoning, collaborates with the ego to make decisions. However, subconscious beliefs and past experiences often influence these decisions, shaping the decision-making process. The guide can also influence our decisions, but we'll explain that more soon.

Identity Construction:
- The ego constructs a sense of identity based on conscious thoughts, self-perception, and external influences. The analytical mind contributes by processing information consciously, while the subconscious provides a repository of past experiences that shape identity.

Defense Mechanisms and Coping Strategies:
- Defense mechanisms employed by the ego to protect self-identity often operate at the subconscious level. The analytical mind may use strategic thinking to justify or rationalize these defense mechanisms.

Introspection and Self-Awareness:
- Introspection, facilitated by the analytical mind, allows individuals to explore and understand subconscious beliefs. This process involves consciously examining automatic thoughts, reactions, and patterns to gain self-awareness. We'll discuss this process more in the Shadow Work chapter.

Challenging and Modifying Beliefs:
- The analytical mind is crucial in challenging and modifying subconscious beliefs. Through critical thinking and intentional reflection, individuals can consciously question and reshape deeply ingrained patterns.

Mindful Observance:
- Mindfulness practices encourage observing thoughts, emotions, and behaviors without immediate judgment. This awareness allows individuals to consciously witness the interplay between the analytical mind and the subconscious.

Role in Emotional Responses:
- Emotional responses, influenced by conscious and subconscious elements, often involve the interplay between the ego and the analytical mind. The subconscious may contribute automatic emotional reactions, while the analytical mind can consciously interpret and respond to these emotions.

Learning and Adaptation:
- The analytical mind facilitates learning from conscious experiences, while the subconscious stores these learnings as automatic responses. The ego adapts its identity and behaviors based on this integrated learning process. This explains how specific tasks we learn can become automatic or second nature without thinking about them. The analytical mind learns a skill, and with enough practice, that skill becomes embedded within our subconscious. The same thing happens with our habits.

We know that was a bit dry, and your brain may hurt trying to process all that (ours sure did in the beginning). We don't expect you to memorize everything said in this chapter, but having a general concept of how the mind works in these ways will help you understand what we discuss throughout the book. We want you to have a basic understanding of everything so there is clarity moving forward. Here's an easy analogy to remember these terms and their relationships with each other: Imagine your mind is like a team working together. The ego is like the leader of this team within the mind, making decisions and helping the analytical mind and subconscious/emotional mind work together. The analytical mind is the tech nerd, always thinking and figuring things out logically. And the subconscious is like the note-taker with a big backpack full of memories and experiences. Imagine that someone says something mean to you. Your leader (ego) might get upset, the tech nerd (analytical mind) thinks about what to do, and the note-taker (subconscious) reminds you of times when you handled similar situations before. So that's how the mind works, but there's one other key ingredient here for the mind, and that's the guide. The guide isn't within the mind but connects the mind to the universal consciousness, to everything and everyone else. And the guide does have a voice. So, let's look at the three voices we hear as observers.

BATTLE OF THE VOICES

🔊 ***EGO***
Fear, Trauma,
Judgement,
& Criticism

🔊 ***ANALYTICAL***
Reason, Problem
Solving,
& Logic

🔊 ***GUIDE***
Love, Intuition,
Passion
& Forgiveness

This figure shows the three voices we hear: the ego, the analytical mind, and the guide. The ego speaks for the subconscious mind since it doesn't have a voice, the analytical mind is purely logical and unemotional, and the guide essentially talks to us about love, intuition, forgiveness, our dreams, etc. Whichever voice we listen to the most is the one that generally wins the battle and speaks the loudest or speaks first when we begin thinking. For many of us, the ego has won the war, so it's often the voice we hear first, most often, and the loudest. The ego can also get involved in a logic debate with others or within ourselves to skew the logic we're trying to discover, figure out, or communicate to someone else. If we let our guide become the loudest and most often listened-to voice out of the 3, we will begin seeing positive changes in our lives. We can let the guide train the ego into not being so upset all the time, releasing negative energy from within the subconscious, thereby making the ego more of a cheerleader instead of a self-sabotager. We'll now begin to break down how the "mind, body, guide" diagram and the "battle of the voices" diagram connect.

So, of the three voices, there's the ego, the only one that complains and is negative. Still, it doesn't always complain, and it's not always negative necessarily. It speaks for the subconscious as well (our emotional memory bank). So, when we are feeling emotional (good or bad), it speaks to what the subconscious is trying to say and what the body is feeling. The analytical mind is the nerd voice that gets things done and figures things out. And then there's the spirit or the guide. This is our connection to the source/universal consciousness/God/quantum realm, whatever you want to call it. This is our inspiration, passion, etc. It guides us toward the person our soul planned for us to be and helps us tap into love and oneness. Now, this figure is called the "battle of the voices." So often, more than one voice is involved in the battle/debate. The ego loves being a bully in these debates. Let's say, for instance, you're trying to figure out how to handle a situation. The ego will cry and scream and say that this situation isn't fair and that you should be upset. The analytical mind will say, "Okay, hold on, what's the rational way to handle this?" and the guide will say, "Handle it with love, forgiveness, and care." We believe the soul is the judge in this battle of the voices, but it wasn't always aware that it was separate from the ego. Typically, it's a debate with no judge, and the ego bullies the rest. You become the judge once you awaken and realize you are the soul/observer. We can become trapped within the ego as the observer and not realize that we are separate from the ego itself. The physical world, stresses of life, and society's stranglehold can cause this. If the soul has a voice, it's the judge's voice and says things like, "Okay, who else wants to take the stand?" and "Okay, this is what we will do based on the debate."

Another way to explain the ego's relationship in this battle is that it tends to act like a nagging neighbor. It's full of itself and wants the world to adjust to what makes it feel good and comfortable. Our ego has attached meaning to everything we've experienced in life. It, therefore, can get triggered and become upset when the outside world pokes at it or brings up a sensitive topic. The topic itself doesn't have to be sensitive; it just brings up the parts of us we disown within our subconscious. When the ego is upset, it will begin nagging and complaining. We must point our awareness (consciousness) at the analytical mind for more rational and logical thoughts to combat the ego. Or we can listen more to our guide (outside of our mind, although it sounds like it's coming from within the mind) and let it speak positivity to combat the negative ego. Our guide always speaks positively. It's like the angel on our shoulder that was shown in cartoons. If the guide is the angel on our shoulders, the devil is often the upset ego.

We want to clarify that the ego isn't always harmful or destructive. It is the source of our self-sabotaging, but the guide can train the ego to help it become more positive and more like a cheerleader rather than the "nagging neighbor." If we don't have many negative/limiting beliefs stored within our subconscious, then the ego doesn't have much to complain about or fear. The analytical mind is more like a computer and has no emotions. The ego can influence the analytical mind, but the analytical mind stays neutral and away from emotion altogether. So, there can be quite the war inside, and we're sure you've noticed this war take place within yourself at some point. Your guide, or even your analytical mind, wants you to change and make better decisions. Still, the ego looks at the subconscious and reads the notes to find that you've never made that change. You've continued to make the same decisions. Hence, the ego fights against the guide and/or analytical voices and tells you that you can't do something or are incapable of positive change. We'll talk about how to help win this battle in later chapters, but for now, let's finish decoding the figures by talking about how the body fits into this equation.

The body is where we store all of our physical feelings. Any physical feeling we end up having is then relayed to the mind, and the mind starts to express this feeling through thoughts. Our emotions within the subconscious can also trigger the body to feel physical sensations. So when you feel sick, your mind tends to start thinking about how unhealthy it feels, how it has or hasn't felt this sickness before. It starts to wonder and even try to predict how long the body may continue to be sick. Even analytical thoughts can bring up feelings in the body. Thoughts and feelings work in tandem. So, suppose you start thinking about being ill or the possibility that you may become sick. In that case, you begin to build up anxiety and stress in the body, which can then turn into a physically ill feeling. This tandem relationship is paramount to understand. Your thoughts affect your feelings, and your feelings affect your thoughts. Also important to note is that your immune system is directly connected to your emotions. When you feel down, depressed, upset, etc., your body begins to release stress hormones, stress proteins, and stress chemicals throughout the body. When you feel happy, excited, joyful, etc., your body releases more healthy hormones, proteins, and chemicals that help your body regenerate and function more normally. This is why the saying "stress kills" holds weight. Stress is what causes sickness, disease, deterioration, etc. Of course, aging slowly deteriorates our bodies, but stress speeds that process up. Knowing that our emotions, thoughts, and feelings affect our energy can help us understand why stress induces sickness and disease. Positive energy makes the body release the right hormones, and vice versa.

The subconscious is what we're not fully aware of within our mind. It's also called our shadow (where our light/awareness does not shine). It contains our notes/records of our emotional history (our beliefs), which is the emotional mind. It also connects the body to the mind. So if we believe something like "I'm not worthy of love" subconsciously, we may not even recognize this about ourselves, and we'll wonder why our thoughts and feelings keep reflecting this negative belief because we aren't aware it lies within our subconscious. The subconscious is what is triggered in the first place. The ego then speaks for it, and the body feels emotions tied to the beliefs the subconscious is expressing. The subconscious doesn't have a voice, but we can hear what it's expressing through the ego and feel it through our body. Our subconscious gathered most of its information in early childhood before our analytical mind was developed. Everything that happened to us in our first 7-12 years of life was absorbed into our subconscious like a sponge with no filter. So, any traumatic experiences we go through end up storing negative beliefs about ourselves here in our subconscious immediately without any filter to keep those negative beliefs at bay. Those beliefs then were either reinforced or released throughout the rest of our lives once we developed a filter (the analytical mind). Still, most negative beliefs we store from childhood go unnoticed for quite a long time until we look inside and notice them. People often think of trauma as something that people who've seen war or were abused experience, yet we all experience trauma as a child. Simply being told to be quiet can make us feel unloved and create trauma. We then feel like speaking up or speaking our minds is no longer viable if we want to be loved. These traumas get stored in our subconscious, and we may never notice them if we ignore what triggers us. Lastly, the guide is our intuition and connection to the source of universal consciousness (God). The guide speaks truth to us and tries to help us understand that life's a bigger picture than our physical self (the ego's self-concept). It will talk to us when we open ourselves up to it. We typically only hear the guide when we feel elevated emotions like love, forgiveness, and gratitude. Sometimes, we seek guidance from this voice when we feel lower emotions, too. The critical thing to note here is that the guide links our mind and the universe. As the observer, we can continue to listen to our guide or our ego more often. Listening to our guide gives us the advice to love life, chase our dreams, and forgive ourselves and others. Listening to our ego tends to place us in a more materialistic or selfish mindset, leading to plenty of negative thinking and, therefore, negative actions. This is a victim mindset. If we listen to the ego too much, we can become trapped within our mind and body and forget that we are the observer of the mind and body. Let's go ahead and explain that in more detail now.

Sometimes, we get stuck in the mind and body, making us forget that we're greater than both. It's like getting trapped in the matrix. We begin thinking our mind and body are the authority or our entire self-identity. Still, we are more significant than both and can control both. As soon as we realize it's just a program, we can understand we don't have to follow it. And then, we can start rewiring the program. It's like being the character in a video game with no control versus being the player of the character in the video game, having complete control.

We are the observers who direct the game's avatar or character (our mind and body). We are not stuck in the matrix of our mind and body. Our guide can lead us in the right direction if we listen to it instead of our thoughts and feelings coming from the matrix. Once we realize our mind and body aren't the authority, we can stop listening to it (the ego) as an authority. We can listen to our ego to know what is wrong within our subconscious and what to change and work on, but we don't have to let it be our authority. It doesn't know what it's talking about, it doesn't have our best interest in mind, it's just been programmed by what we've experienced in life, and it just keeps running the same programs. There's nothing wrong with that objectively; it's doing its job, but it's time to retrain our mind and body (the avatar) to live a better life. We're no longer programming our mind and body to stress us out; we reprogram it to heal and make us feel great. Our guide is what can flip the switch and start redirecting our mind and body to the right path of thinking and feeling. We can listen more to the guide so that the guide begins rewiring our programs and habits into better versions. We are observers, though, so we don't have to feel negative about ourselves just because our avatar isn't the best or has the best habits. We are fantastic as we are. That means we can do better or start developing better habits. But if we decide to continue believing the lie that we're only ever going to be good enough when we accomplish something spectacular, are praised by many, or become successful, then we most likely will never be able to feel great about ourselves. Don't let the avatar's troubles affect your self-esteem as the observer. Have good self-esteem and self-worth now so that you can confidently begin changing your habits and look forward to becoming better instead of feeling the need to be better to feel happy and worthy. See that the trauma you've endured programmed negative/limiting beliefs into your subconscious to make you feel less than whole. This forced you to become inauthentic and hide away the parts of you that you decided to disown. You were worthy and whole the whole time, but trauma made you feel otherwise.

Let's discuss how the battle of the voices involves willpower and decision-making. The concept of willpower and the decision-making process can involve a combination of the ego, analytical mind, and the inner voice of intuition or our guide.

Ego:
- The ego can influence decisions based on desires, fears, and external validation. It often seeks immediate gratification and may only sometimes align with long-term goals.

Analytical Mind:
- The analytical mind plays a role in decision-making by assessing pros and cons, considering logical implications, and analyzing information. It tends to be rational and objective.

Spirit/Guide:
- The inner voice associated with the spirit guide or our higher self represents a more profound, intuitive knowing. This voice often aligns with a sense of purpose, higher values, and a broader perspective beyond immediate desires.

Willpower:
- Willpower is often associated with the ability to make conscious choices and resist impulses. It can draw from various sources, including the determination of the ego, the reasoned decisions of the analytical mind, and the guidance of the inner voice.

Final Verdict:
- The final verdict in decision-making may involve harmonizing these voices. In this context, Willpower is the ability to align decisions with a more profound sense of purpose, values, and long-term vision, which the intuitive voice may guide within.

Ultimately, individuals may experience this process differently, and the interplay of these voices can vary based on personal beliefs, experiences, and levels of self-awareness. The dynamic interaction of these aspects contributes to the complexity of decision-making and the exercise of Willpower.

So, what's the takeaway from this chapter? We are the cause of our stress, no one or nothing else. Situations and other people may influence us to feel stressed or happy. Still, ultimately, our mind truly affects us and decides how we interpret our reality. If we can learn to understand this within ourselves, we can start the journey of change. If we don't understand this about ourselves, then we're doomed to continue being a slave to our minds and bodies. Our mind and body will dictate what we think and feel and, therefore, what we do. Understanding that we (the observer) are the master and controller of the mind and body can help us break free from the chains with which the mind and body bind us. Knowing we are the observer helps us understand that we don't have to listen to the nagging neighbor (ego). Instead, we can direct our thoughts and feelings in whichever direction we choose. We can't stop the mind and body from reacting, but we can choose not to decide to act upon these reactions. We can pause, gather our rational and positive thoughts, and then respond to each situation more clearly instead of instantly choosing to react however the body and mind tell us to. Allowing the guide to speak up can help us dilute the ego's complaints and lead us down a brighter path toward a happier and more fulfilling life. In time, we can rewire our subconscious so that the ego no longer has such a negative view of our past. This will make the ego not complain, fear, worry, etc., nearly as much. We'll discuss this in more detail later in the book. We will continue analyzing the ego and how it currently affects our decisions. We covered the basics in this chapter, so let's take a deep dive into the ego in this next chapter.

CHAPTER 6: THE EGO

In this chapter, we will peel back the layers of the ego to uncover the nuances of its influence on our lives. We aim to recognize the ego and its intricate workings and empower ourselves to navigate beyond its limitations. We will explain the techniques of overcoming the ego more in other chapters, but for now, we'd like to introduce some of these techniques to build upon later. We like the analogy of thinking of our mind as three radio stations or TV channels. The ego is the drama channel full of controversy and relationship turbulence, the analytical mind is the DIY channel full of skills and knowledge of the world around us, and the guide is the fantasy channel full of our dreams, wants, and desires. So, let's get to know the drama queen we call our ego.

The ego was once necessary to help us grow. Still, now it's threatening our survival because it's often triggering us, lowering our energy, and placing us in a primal state of fight/flight due to its sensitivity and fragility. So it is utterly vital to understand the role it's playing in our minds and our lives. It's affecting not only our well-being but also the people around us and the situations we have in our lives. The urgency lies in deciphering the ego's role, understanding its impact, and developing strategies to liberate ourselves from its grasp. Picture the ego as a sculptor, crafting a false version of yourself using the raw material of thoughts and feelings. This pseudo-self forms based on your perceptions and reactions to the ever-evolving world around you. While initially essential for personal growth, the ego becomes a self-imposed limitation, urging us to transcend its illusory constructs. When we understand our ego as the mind of our avatar, not ourselves, we can begin lowering the volume of the ego so there's more space for the guide and the analytical mind to thrive. The ego isn't always negative, but it is the only part of our mind that complains, yells, screams, and gets upset. The subconscious mind is what the ego speaks for, so technically, the subconscious is upset, but the ego is the voice.

In contrast to the self-identity the ego has created, your true self lies in your soul. Our soul is who we are; the soul doesn't care about worldly things, self-image, our job, or anything. If you lost everything, the ego would be devastated, but the soul wouldn't be phased. So, visualize life as a vast playground where your body, thoughts, and accumulated knowledge are essential tools for navigating the intricate game of existence. These tools are crucial, yet they don't make up your identity. Despite surface-level differences, all egos share a fundamental structure comprising fear, desire, comparison, greed, and other intrinsic traits it gathers from the subconscious mind. The ego's need for contrast and division becomes evident as individuals compare themselves based on appearance, background, or skills. Recognizing this fundamental sameness beneath apparent differences is the first step toward liberation. We are all one when we remove our self-identity, but we do need our self-identity to progress through life as this avatar. However, becoming solely focused on self-identity, especially to generate self-esteem, self-worth, and self-confidence, is a losing battle in the long run—those things we should already have regardless of our appearance, job, background, skills, etc.

Acknowledging the impersonal nature of the conditioned mind, we uncover the truth that egoic patterns are not unique to individuals. Instead, they share a collective thread that binds the human experience. Viewing events and egoic patterns without attaching personal labels transforms them into impartial facts of the moment. This recognition frees us from the shackles of ego-driven judgments, fostering a sense of understanding and forgiveness. Rather than perceiving events through a personal lens, they become universal phenomena, transcending the constraints of individual identity. This shift in perspective transforms our approach to life, fostering positive contributions to the collective consciousness. We can change our perspective by understanding that our ego speaks much louder and has more influence when we feel pain in the body. Embracing our pain with acceptance and forgiveness allows us to bypass what the ego says to better listen to the spirit/guide.

An essential practice on the path to ego transcendence is accepting the present moment without resistance. Recognizing the power of now and aligning with its flow becomes an ally in the journey toward self-realization. By forgiving ourselves and others, we begin paving the way for surrender to the natural unfolding of life. Contrary to misconceptions, surrender is not synonymous with resignation. It involves allowing the present moment to be as it is without imposing resistance. In this act of surrender, true strength reveals itself. Focusing on the now becomes a natural outcome of this surrender, ushering in inner peace and spiritual power. We discover that resistance is futile, and genuine strength lies in accepting and surrendering to what is. In later chapters, we'll get into techniques for staying present in the moment and how to forgive. For now, we want to mention a few more things to know about the ego.

Being present in the moment involves a heightened awareness of the simple things surrounding us. We cultivate the presence of the mind by focusing on our thoughts, feelings, and bodily sensations. This practice extends to daily tasks, emphasizing the integration of awareness into every aspect of our lives. Central to the process of overcoming the ego is the realization that you are consciousness itself, distinct from the transient thoughts and reactions of the mind. Liberating yourself from the damaging commentary generated by the mind becomes pivotal. This practice encourages a focus on deeper feelings and an acute awareness of the present moment, paving the way for a profound connection with the essence of being. Suffering emerges as a potential teacher, guiding us toward enlightenment. Rather than being viewed as impediments, loss and challenges become gateways to spiritual realization. The key lies in embracing awareness, staying present, and recognizing the transformative potential in every suffering moment. So, how do we begin implementing these strategies on a basic level?

Overcoming The Ego:

Engage in profound listening:
- Dive into the practice of deep listening, devoid of judgment. Create a sacred space for understanding beyond mere thoughts and emotions. By cultivating an intense presence, you establish a profound connection with others, refraining from validating negative narratives. This sets the stage for unraveling the ego's grip on interpersonal dynamics.

Cultivate mind pattern awareness:
- Stay vigilant in swiftly identifying and bringing unobserved thought patterns into the light of consciousness. Utilize meditation as a tool to clear the mind, verbalize thoughts while maintaining detachment, and remain alert to recurring negative mental patterns. This heightened awareness serves as a compass for navigating the labyrinth of the egoic mind.

Use memory as a learning tool:
- View memories as valuable tools for learning without succumbing to psychological suffering. Treat memories as video footage, providing a more comfortable environment for heightened awareness of the ego's patterns. This shift in perspective transforms memories from burdens to valuable insights on the path to ego transcendence.

Practice acceptance and allowance:
- Embrace phrases such as "I accept" or "I allow," synchronized with breathing, to foster a mindset of acceptance. Acknowledge challenges in accepting and, if needed, take appropriate action without resisting the present moment. This practice invites a harmonious coexistence with the flow of life, dismantling the ego's resistance.

Watch the ego's reactions:
- Recognize the futility of resisting undesirable stimuli and cultivate a witnessing presence. Redirect attention to the present moment anchors when egoic reactions arise in response to unpleasant situations or thoughts. This practice empowers you to break free from the automatic, ego-driven responses perpetuating suffering.

Monitor physical reactions:
- Observe physical responses, such as tension or movement, associated with undesirable thoughts or situations. Stay vigilant to subtle physical reactions, preventing the unconscious perpetuation of self-destructive patterns. This physical awareness acts as a mirror reflecting the ego's influence on both the mind and body.

Embrace conceptual freedom:
- Embrace the formless and unconditioned nature of genuine intelligence, moving beyond the constraints of conceptual thinking. This conceptual freedom opens the door to a holistic and unbounded self-understanding.

Meditate for present awareness:
- Engage in meditation during daily activities, focusing on breath, thoughts, inner body, and sense perceptions to stay grounded in the present moment. Whether structured or unstructured, meditation becomes a continuous practice, fostering heightened awareness throughout various aspects of daily life.

The ego accesses the records of our past within our subconscious. The goal is to rewrite these records eventually through self-transformation. Finally, the ego will change its self-concept because the subconscious records will not have any negative beliefs left inside to hold us back. This will prevent us from self-sabotaging. The ego won't have negative beliefs that distort its self-concept of itself, so it will eventually become a confident, positive, and healthy ego. We'll learn how to release these negative/limiting beliefs later in the book, but we want you to know this is the end goal. We must create some distance from the ego, establish control over it, and eventually forgive our past so that the ego can let go of the negativity we're carrying inside our subconscious. As much as we'd like to demonize the ego, it speaks for our subconscious. So, without the ego, we may never be able to discover our limiting beliefs. For this, we thank the ego for its functionality. The first step is creating separation between yourself and your ego. Do your best not to react to things and give yourself time to let the other two voices speak reason to you before you react. That's the difference between reacting and responding. A response requires more of a thought process. Reacting is choosing to say or do the first thing that comes to mind regardless of how that choice may affect yourself and others. Now that we've expanded on the ego and explained that it is the main culprit holding us back in our transformation journey, we want to start explaining the first M out of the 4 Ms. We briefly covered it earlier. Still, it's time to dive into it and show you how it helps change perspective, which will change your life.

CHAPTER 7: MATTER IS ENERGY

Here we are, seven chapters in, and finally getting to the first M. What's the matter with us? Matter matters because it's what we are made up of. But what is matter made up of? Energy, obviously, you were paying attention, right? Energy is not only what makes up our entire being but also what makes up the entire universe. Energy is even present where matter is not. This means that energy is the critical component we must understand and use to keep our mind and body functioning at their highest level. So what's the matter with our energy? Well, negative energy creates stress, and positive energy heals the body from the stress it previously created. What needs to be understood is that any chronic condition we may develop is developed because of sustained negative energy in our body for an extended period. We cause ourselves to have chronic conditions, so only we can heal ourselves from those same chronic conditions that we generated in the first place. Even some diseases or conditions caused by an outside source can be cured in the body through sustained positive energy. So, the critical component to living your best life is maintaining positive energy. Science has made strides in this area, pointing to positivity's healing power. The science of energy can now explain miraculous medical recoveries via quantum physics and neuroscience. We recommend Joe Dispenza for this research, but countless others in the same field have the same conclusions. The key is embracing new emotions and vivid images to forge a path towards your best self.

"So, positive energy matters? You're saying all I have to do is be positive, and I'll become healthy and live my best life?" Our answer would be a resounding Yes! Being positive all the time isn't as easy as it sounds, though, especially if you're an adult and have all kinds of trauma that you haven't dealt with. These traumas hide in our subconscious mind and can be challenging to detect if you don't know how to become aware of them. Let's start this awareness process by describing positive versus negative energy.

Positive energy is not necessarily more powerful than negative energy but carries a higher vibrational frequency. This also means positive emotions have a higher vibrational frequency than negative emotions. Our thoughts and feelings create the energy that vibrates within us. That energy also radiates outwards from our body and mind. This is why you hear certain sayings like "killing the vibe" when discussing spreading negative energy. Suppose someone was vibrating at an extremely high frequency, and they allowed someone else's lower vibrational energy to affect their energy. In that case, it's lowering the vibration within them. You can find plenty of emotional energy charts out there, and we remade a simple version of this chart below. This meter is how we like to think of our energy at any given moment visually. The more we can stay high on this meter with high-frequency vibrations, the better off we will be in our lives. So, the idea is to channel and sustain elevated emotions, which give off high frequencies, as often as possible.

So, anytime throughout your day, you may wonder where that arrow is. "Am I feeling and thinking low vibes or high vibes? And if they're low, then how do I get them back up?" That arrow determines our reality. Our personality is what makes up our personal reality. Our personality is how we think, feel, and act. "What you think, you become. What you feel, you attract. What you imagine, you create." -Buddha. So, in any situation, the reality of the situation is determined by how we think, feel, and act. The same problem we deal with daily can become a negative or a positive reality based on how our energy vibrates when the situation occurs. And we can shift that reality by moving the arrow in either direction.

For instance, you start a conversation with someone, and that arrow is in the middle. You're not feeling positive or negative, just in the middle somewhere. If someone says something that triggers a negative feeling within you, which causes some negative thoughts, our arrow immediately moves toward a negative reality. We can then realize that just because our mind and body want that arrow to begin sliding towards an adverse reaction, creating a negative experience and reality, doesn't mean we have to abide by what our mind and body want us to do. We can pull that arrow back to the center by zoning out and becoming present by focusing our energy elsewhere. Or better yet, we can focus on our heart if we want to pull the arrow back to the positive. Let the heart find forgiveness for yourself, that person, and the experience of feeling and thinking negatively. This is how we release negative emotions and go back to being able to feel elevated emotions. We'll cover that more in detail later in the book.

If we fight that negative energy, we're giving it power. If we fear that negative energy, we let it take over because we're too afraid to battle it. Instead, we can notice it and accept that it's there. We can realize it needs to be released. So, we turn that negative energy over to our hearts and forgive ourselves for lowering our frequency. Doing that can remove that negative energy instead of surprising it. Then it releases, and we feel lighter and much more full of positive energy. If we focus on the heart, that arrow will go from forgiveness and acceptance to joy, relief, gratitude, etc. If you can do it once, you'll feel how good it feels to let that negative energy go—not suppressing it but embracing and releasing it. "Here it is; it's trying to let me know it's been built up for some time now. If I ignore or fear it; it'll be stronger next time. Or I can accept it, forgive it, and let it go. That way, negative energy becomes less of a burden, making it weaker the next time it appears." That first release has the most resistance, just like whenever we try to do anything for the first time. But if we can accomplish it once, the second and third times are much more manageable. Eventually, this tedious process goes from being a chore to transforming into curiosity. You may eventually say something like, "Wow! I feel so much better after getting rid of many built-up negative emotions. What else can I release? What's left in there? I want to find it all and free it all because it feels so great taking that weight off my body." The first step is becoming aware of our thoughts and feelings, though. Then, learning not to react. We'll have to work up to being able to forgive. We may be providing spoilers here, that forgiveness is the key, but we just want to make sure you know there's more to the process than simply becoming aware and learning to not react.

So, our reality is based on where we are on that meter. And it changes throughout the day, usually because we allow the outside world to dictate which part of the meter we're on. Someone cuts us off in traffic, and that meter moves down. Someone compliments us, and that meter moves up. Eventually, we realize that waiting for the outside world to affect and change our energy meter is no way to live. We're then a victim of the situations that happen in our lives. Why wait for something positive to happen to us to feel positive, though? "Don't wait for an experience to feel an emotion. That's cause and effect. Feeling the emotion ahead of the experience is causing the effect." -Dr Joe Dispenza. So, cause the effect by feeling great now and as often as possible. We want to reiterate that no situation will ever be better handled with negative energy than positive energy in your everyday life. That negative energy ends up sending us into survival mode. It's fight or flight or flee. This instinct was perfect for our tribal and caveman days, but it's not nearly as helpful today. We don't experience danger nearly as frequently, so our fight, flight, or free response can do us more harm than good. Becoming aware of when it's happening and what to do to counter it is a vital part of living your best life. "Your life does not get better by chance; it gets better by change," Jim Rohn said. Let's consider a few more situations and explain how positivity will always yield a better result.

Imagine two candidates awaiting their turn for a job interview. Candidate A is positive and confident and speaks highly of their skills and experiences. Candidate B, however, adopts a negative approach, expressing doubt about their qualifications and complaining about the job market. Naturally drawn to positivity, the interviewer perceives Candidate A as the better fit for the team, as they bring an optimistic and solution-oriented mindset.

In a collaborative work environment, a team faces a challenging project. Team Member A embraces a positive attitude, encouraging creativity and emphasizing the strengths of each team member. On the other hand, Team Member B approaches the task with negativity, highlighting potential failures and dwelling on problems. The project encounters setbacks, but the team's positive energy allows them to overcome obstacles more effectively than if they had succumbed to negativity.

Consider a couple facing a disagreement. Partner A adopts a positive approach, seeking compromise and expressing gratitude for the relationship. Meanwhile, Partner B responds negatively, criticizing and dwelling on past grievances. Over time, Partner A's positive outlook fosters a healthier relationship, while Partner B's negativity contributes to further discord.

Let's say you're walking, and a bee buzzes near you. If you fear it, the energy you create from worrying about it projects into your reality. You're now living in a moment where your mind says you must fear this bee because it may harm you. You are now being attacked and chased by a bee in your mind. Now, let's look at the actual reality of this situation. Most of the time, bees aren't aggressive and won't attack. The same goes for most living things. They only attack when they feel the need to defend themselves or if they are hunting. Bees don't chase us, though.
We provoked that bee by swatting at it, its home, or its family. And it will feel no need to risk its life by attacking you if you didn't provoke it and make it feel the need to defend. Imagine the same walk, but you're pleased and grateful this time. The same bee comes along, and you barely even notice it. If you notice it, you begin to see it as a bee, admire it for its beauty or flying ability, or just as another living thing in this vast universe you can feel connected to. Your reality at that moment is entirely the opposite of the person who feared the bee. Still, the objective reality was that a bee was near you. It wasn't attacking you, and it wasn't trying to connect with you or communicate necessarily. It's just doing its thing. So, if you're a person who lets your fear of bees change your reality every time a bee is nearby, then you'll keep living in that kind of fight/flight reality. And if you're a person who isn't afraid of bees, you'll never live in that reality. These realities only happen because we attach an emotion to them. The typical reality has no feeling and is only logic. It says it's just a bee near me, nothing more, because that's all it is. Our emotions put a lens over our eyes, changing the reality of what is happening.

Responding with negativity, even towards negativity, doesn't yield the results we want. "Eye for an eye" and "fighting fire with fire" aren't healthy responses. Most people have learned this the hard way, but only some have. We can't think of any interaction we've ever had that wouldn't have been better to respond positively, be it understanding, empathy, kindness, etc. If someone is being rude to you, you will only make matters worse by being rude back to them. Positive energy always wins in the end against negative energy. See, negative energy is tense. It isn't stable. It has to let go at some point. The tension has to be released. And the only thing that keeps that tension going is more tension. Negativity fuels negativity. Positive energy is not tense and, therefore, can keep flowing freely.

Many, if not all of us writing this book, used to think that if we just knocked someone out, we'd be doing them and everyone else a favor, and they'd learn their lesson. But it never yields the results we want. First of all, it risks jail time and physical danger. But beyond the risks, it isn't as effective in achieving the desired outcome in the first place. Punching that person may become a significant clue for them to finally look into the mirror and see that they should change. Still, it won't be the sole reason they change, if they do at all. Most will adopt a victim mindset and decide not to learn the lesson we want them to learn. And in the meantime, it won't be better for their immediate growth or situation. Trying to show them empathy and let them know that we understand where they're coming from and that we can relate is a much better approach. Calm someone down without making them feel attacked or belittled. Let them see that they let their emotions get the best of them and that it will be okay. We stand a much better shot at fixing the situation and possibly helping them learn a lesson with the positive approach, and we risk nothing.

The negative response is never the better one. And it sounds so cheesy and superficial. These simple phrases may make us think, "Yeah, yeah, you sound like my first-grade teacher or my mom," but they are too true. Being negative back to someone is going to solve the issue. The old "eye for an eye" mentality. "They're rude, so I will be rude to back." That only fuels the fire, though. Negativity fuels negativity. Positivity doesn't give negativity fuel. So that negativity will have to cease if no other negativity is present to fuel it. Negativity can cloud the light of positivity and win, but that's only if we let positivity give up. Positivity will win that battle in the long and usually even in the short run. It will never need to give up. Our ego is what convinces us to give up the positivity. Negativity is too tense; it has to loosen up at some point. Positivity has no tensing it up, so it can keep shining as long as it wants.

Now that we see that negativity solves nothing and is much less effective than positivity, it will become easy for us to see the positive path and choose a favorable option with everything in life. Why let anything bother us? We can feel wonderful, in love with the world, love ourselves, and feel whole. We don't need anything; we love life. Will we partake in the spoils of life? Yes, but without letting the spoils make us addicted to this physical world. The real world is inside of us. True happiness is inside of us, and we can visit anytime. And we don't have to leave. We always want to see life positively, choose positive actions, think positive thoughts, and feel elevated energy. This is how we heal and how we grow.

Choosing to forgive instead and approaching the situation with love, understanding, and empathy will always yield better results. With other people, when dealing with ourselves, and even when trying to accomplish things like tasks. We're much more productive when we have a positive mindset. If we feel great when we do a task, we will get it done much better, and it won't feel like a chore because we're feeling great. We'll figure out how we can make that mundane task fun. Music while we do it, A little dance step? Challenging ourselves to do the task faster or better than usual can be fun. Or even just tuning out while we do it and appreciating all it offers. Think about how small we are in this universe and yet how connected we are. We are all energy. We are made of the same thing and come from the same place.

Negativity needs fuel for its fire. So now think of that same scenario of someone being rude. Still, this time, they're being rude to a positive person who is just trying to help the negative person. The negative person can only keep it up for so long before they give in. Eventually, they'll have to settle down and let that positive energy in. You can picture this battle of energies like Harry Potter when he's facing Voldemort...oops... "He Who Shall Not Be Named." Their magic energy meeting in the middle and trying to push back the other is much like the energy we give off. Energy is contagious. So, will you allow other's negative energy to ruin your positive energy? After reading this entire book, we hope you'll realize that being negative does no good for anyone. It hurts others, and it hurts yourself. Even being spiteful or having resentment is horrible for us. "Resentment is like drinking poison and expecting our enemies to die." In reality, all you're doing is poisoning yourself. So let's work on getting rid of that negative energy so there's more room for positive energy to flow through us.

Life can be as beautiful as we choose it to be or as horrible as we choose it to be. That decision is made within the mind and is expressed through the body, then outwardly expelled to those around us as energy. Again, energy is contagious. And it's very tough to continue being negative towards someone who won't budge on being positive. The negative always submits as long as the positive energy isn't wavered. How long have you ever been able to be mad at someone who refused to be mad back at you and just wanted to help you feel well again? We know that even on our worst negative days, we can't stay mad at someone who's only expelling positive energy toward us. The only thing that fuels that fire of negativity is more negativity. So, which side of the meter would you like to spend most of your reality?

CHAPTER 8: MEDITATION

Here is the second M, Meditation. This is the most effective first step towards making a change within yourself. Meditation means to become aware of oneself. That's all it is. We know that some people have odd feelings towards meditation and feel like it's not something that they'd ever do. You may think it's just something that spiritual people do or that monks practice. You may see it as a waste of time, but we assure you that it's none of those things. So allow us to explain the benefits we all receive from meditating. Here's the thing about meditation: it can be for a short time, and it doesn't matter what kind of meditation you do. All meditations involve relaxing into your body and clearing your mind at first. There are many different guided meditations out there that have different uses, but they all start by relaxing and clearing your mind. This exact practice of relaxing and clearing your mind is what we want to practice so you can get used to pushing thoughts away from your consciousness. If you can get good at this without distractions besides your mind and body, you can start implementing these same tactics in your daily life. That act is called being present or becoming mindful, and we'll get to that later, but for now, we would like to introduce you to this great habit. It's such a simple habit; it doesn't take much dedication or commitment, and you'll feel better every time you do it.

We're so distracted by the world these days. Everything is instant; we get dopamine rushes from countless things, and we're constantly putting our attention everywhere except the present moment. Meditation is a gift to ourselves. Try to see it as a personal vacation or a one-on-one date with yourself. The end goal here is to love yourself. When you love yourself, you're going to love life as well. So, the main thing that is accomplished when we meditate is relaxation, but many great things happen to the mind and body in the process of slowing everything down for a moment. Side effects most likely include, but are not limited to, reduced stress, improved focus, and concentration, increased emotional stability, enchanted awareness of self, greater creativity, better sleep, increased resilience against stress, improved cardiovascular health, enhanced immune function, increased pain tolerance and pain management, improved respiratory function, reduced inflammation, more balanced hormones, fewer mood swings, and becoming one's best self. It's incredible what this simple exercise does for people, and it's just the beginning of the journey.

Meditation is essentially training wheels for self-improvement. 5/5 stars, we highly recommend. This is where it all starts. If you can sit down and be comfortable with yourself for a few minutes, you'll learn how to be comfortable with yourself throughout the day. We will show you the seven energy centers or chakras most meditations mention. This picture explains what each energy center contains and what blocks each energy center.

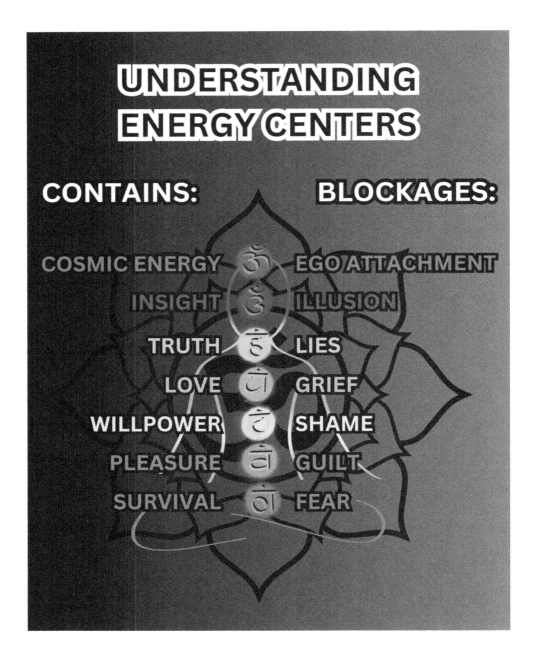

As you see, our body has seven chakras/energy centers. We can better understand our body by understanding what types of emotions block each center. We can also help our energy flow more smoothly through our bodies by freeing up those blockages with meditation. Our traumas and other negativity get caught within our bodies. That energy becomes stuck in one or more of our energy centers. By aligning them with focused meditation, we can help release those blockages.

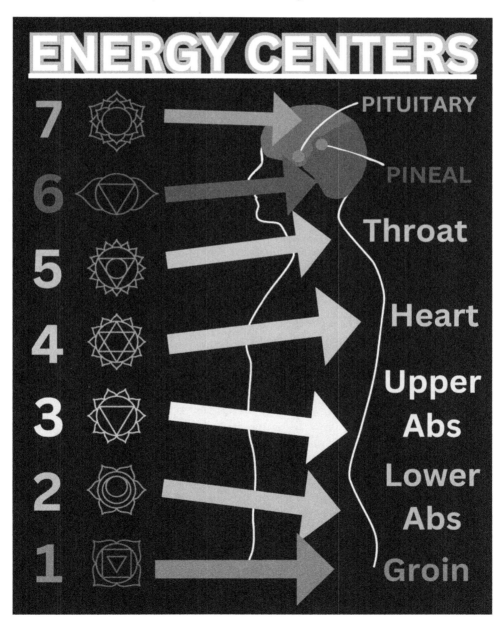

If you've ever seen a chakra diagram, it looks similar to the first diagram. It reveals a person in a meditation pose and facing forward. People tend to get confused about the brain's 6th and 7th energy centers. If you've ever looked at a diagram of the brain, then you've seen that the pituitary gland is lower in the brain than the pineal gland. And yet, the pituitary gland is considered to reside in the 7th energy center, above the 6th energy center. And the pineal gland is considered to reside in the 6th energy center. So how can this be? In a simple chart showing the human body from a frontal view, it then seems like the 6th energy center is the space between our nose and throat, and the 7th energy center is the space between our nose and the top of the head. However, this is not the truth. Instead, the 6th center, containing the pineal gland, starts from the back of the head, where the neck meets the skull and expands upwards and forward through half of the brain, encompassing the pineal gland. The 7th center then starts and expands from the pituitary gland, in the center of the brain, to the crown/top of the head. So, if you want to sense your 6th energy center, focus your energy near the back of the head where the neck meets the bottom of the skull. If you want to sense your 7th energy center, focus your energy behind your eyes. This is why they call the 7th center your "third eye." Each one of these energy centers has its own torus field of energy. So imagine seven separate torus fields up and down your entire body. Some teach that the 6th center encompasses the head as a whole and includes both the pituitary and pineal glands within it. This makes the 7th center just above the head as a connection to the quantum field. Really, either description for the 6th and 7th center works to help understand our energy within. The slight differences in teachings shouldn't change much.

There are many types of meditations done by many different kinds of teachers and spiritual leaders. Just because you meditate doesn't mean you have to be a spiritual person, but it does tend to go hand in hand. The more aware you become of yourself, the closer to the divine you tend to be. What you name that divine and how you describe it doesn't matter, but having some relationship with yourself and, by proxy, with the sacred is excellent. God, the universe, the source, quantum energy, universal energy, universal consciousness, etc. They're all within us. It is within every one of us because we all came from the same place, and we are all made up of the same thing. We are all from the same cloth. We are all energy. Energy can not be created or destroyed; it can only be transferred or transformed.

Here's a long list of various types of meditations, along with their purposes:

Mindfulness Meditation:
- **Purpose:** Cultivating present-moment awareness, reducing stress, and improving focus.

Loving-Kindness Meditation (Metta):
- **Purpose:** Cultivating feelings of love and compassion toward oneself and others.

Body Scan Meditation:
- **Purpose:** Developing awareness of bodily sensations, promoting relaxation, and reducing tension.

Breath Awareness Meditation:
- **Purpose:** Focusing on the breath to cultivate mindfulness, reduce anxiety, and enhance concentration.

Transcendental Meditation (TM):
- **Purpose:** Achieving a state of restful awareness and promoting inner calm.

Zen Meditation (Zazen):
- **Purpose:** Attaining insight into the nature of the mind and reality through sitting meditation.

Chakra Meditation:
- **Purpose:** Balancing and aligning the body's energy centers (chakras) for overall well-being.

Guided Meditation:
- **Purpose:** Following the guidance of a teacher or recorded script to achieve specific outcomes, such as relaxation or personal growth.

Mantra Meditation:
- **Purpose:** Repetition of a mantra to focus the mind, promote concentration, and access higher states of consciousness.

Walking Meditation:
- **Purpose:** Integrating mindfulness into movement, fostering awareness, and promoting relaxation.

Vipassana Meditation:
- **Purpose:** Developing insight into the impermanence and interconnectedness of all phenomena.

Yoga Nidra:
- **Purpose:** A state of conscious relaxation, promoting deep rest and stress reduction.

Body Awareness Meditation:
- **Purpose:** Bringing attention to sensations, promoting a mind-body connection, and reducing tension.

Compassion Meditation:
- **Purpose:** Cultivating feelings of compassion toward oneself and others.

Deep Breathing Meditation:
- **Purpose:** Utilizing slow and intentional breaths to induce relaxation and reduce stress.

Silent Meditation:
- **Purpose:** Practicing mindfulness and self-awareness in silence.

Visualization Meditation:
- **Purpose:** Creating mental images to promote relaxation, focus, or manifestation.

Gratitude Meditation:
- **Purpose:** Focusing on and expressing gratitude for positive aspects of life.

Sound Bath Meditation:
- **Purpose:** Experiencing healing and relaxation through the use of sound, often using singing bowls or gongs.

Compassion-Focused Meditation:
- **Purpose:** Cultivating a sense of compassion toward oneself and others.

Inner Child Meditation:
- **Purpose:** Connecting with and healing the inner child for emotional well-being.

Sufi Whirling Meditation:
- **Purpose:** Combining spinning movements with mindfulness to induce a trance-like state and spiritual insight.

Energy Clearing Meditation:
- **Purpose:** Clearing and balancing personal energy for emotional and physical well-being.

Mindful Eating Meditation:
- **Purpose:** Bringing full awareness to the act of eating for a mindful and healthy relationship with food.

Gratitude Journaling Meditation:
- **Purpose:** Combining meditation with journaling to reflect on and express gratitude.

Remember that individuals may resonate differently with various meditation practices, and it's beneficial to explore different types to find what works best for personal needs and preferences. This list of meditations doesn't even cover every type of meditation. As you can see, there are countless things to be accomplished with this beautiful practice. Each meditation has a different purpose, but they all accomplish similar things. Even the specific frequency used in recorded meditations has a purpose. The words in meditations draw our attention and energy to things like our body, mind, space around us, past, future, etc. So the real question is, what do you want from your next mediation?

Sometimes, meditating without a guided voice track is better, especially for your first time. You don't want it to feel too much like a chore. Guidance is lovely, especially in the beginning when you're learning new techniques within meditation. Eventually, you'll want to be no longer distracted by guidance and be with yourself to explore yourself better. This is also a better practice for your daily life because you can listen to music or meditations throughout the day. Still, you'll have to experience life without a tool that helps you keep your energy high and positive. When you can control your emotions and thoughts without external stimuli, you're now in control of your life, and you won't need external things as a crutch to keep you happy. You'll be pleased with yourself, by yourself, just by using just the tools that you have inside. Let's now discuss some breathwork that can aid you in your meditation.

Breathwork:

1. Diaphragmatic Breathing:
Instructions:
- Inhale deeply through your nose, expanding your diaphragm, allowing your abdomen to rise. Exhale slowly through your mouth, feeling your abdomen fall.
Benefits:
- Enhances oxygen exchange, reduces stress, and promotes relaxation.
2. Equal Breathing:
Instructions:
- Inhale and exhale for an equal count (e.g., inhale for 4, exhale for 4). Maintain a steady rhythm.
Benefits:
- Encourages balance, focus, and relaxation by syncing breath with a consistent pattern.

3. Box Breathing:
Instructions:
- Inhale for a count, hold for the same count, exhale, and then pause before the next inhalation (e.g., 4-4-4-4).
Benefits:
- Calms the nervous system, improves focus and reduces anxiety.

4. 4-7-8 Breathing (Relaxing Breath):
Instructions:
- Inhale for four counts, hold for seven counts, and exhale for eight. Repeat for several cycles.
Benefits:
- Induces relaxation, eases tension, and helps with sleep.

5. Alternate Nostril Breathing (Nadi Shodhana):
Instructions:
- Close one nostril, inhale through the other, switch nostrils, exhale. Repeat, alternating nostrils.
Benefits:
- Balances energy, reduces stress and enhances focus.

6. Ujjayi Breath:
Instructions:
- Constrict the back of your throat to create a subtle, ocean-like sound during inhalation and exhalation.
Benefits:
- Calms the mind, warms the body, and fosters mindfulness.

7. Kapalabhati (Fire Breath):
Instructions:
- Forceful exhales by contracting the abdomen rapidly, with passive inhales. Start slowly and gradually increase speed.
Benefits:
- Boosts energy, clears the mind and strengthens the abdominal muscles.

8. Bhramari (Bee Breath):
Instructions:
- Inhale deeply and exhale with a humming sound, prolonging the exhalation.
Benefits:
- Relieves stress, calms the nervous system and promotes a sense of tranquility.

9. Anapanasati:

Instructions:

- Observe the natural breath without altering it. Focus on the sensation of breath at the nostrils or abdomen.

Benefits:

- Enhances mindfulness, concentration, and self-awareness.

10. Three-Part Breath (Dirga Pranayama):

Instructions:

- Inhale deeply into the abdomen, expand the ribcage, and finally fill the chest. Exhale in reverse order.

Benefits:

- Increases lung capacity, promotes relaxation, and balances energy.

11. Sitali (Cooling Breath):

Instructions:

- Inhale through a rolled tongue or puckered lips, creating a cooling effect. Exhale through the nose.

Benefits:

- Cools the body, reduces stress, and calms the nervous system.

12. Buteyko Breathing:

Instructions:

- Emphasizes nasal breathing and slowing down the breath to reduce volume.

Benefits:

- Improves respiratory function, reduces anxiety, and enhances overall well-being.

13. Holotropic Breathwork:

Instructions:

- Deep and rhythmic breathing to induce altered states of consciousness. Often guided in a therapeutic setting.

Benefits:

- Facilitates emotional release, spiritual exploration, and self-discovery.

14. Zen Buddhist Breath Counting:

Instructions:

- Inhale and exhale naturally, counting each exhalation to a specific number before starting again.

Benefits:

- Cultivates mindfulness, focus, and concentration.

15. Mindful Breath Awareness:
Instructions:
- Observe the natural breath without altering it. Bring attention back to the breath when the mind wanders.
Benefits:
- Cultivates mindfulness, reduces stress and enhances overall well-being

16. Wim Hof Method:
Instructions:
- This technique involves a cycle of deep, rapid breaths followed by a breath hold. Inhale deeply through the nose, exhale fully through the mouth, and repeat rapidly. After several rounds, take a final deep breath, exhale, and hold for as long as it is comfortable. When you need to breathe, inhale deeply and hold for 15 seconds, then exhale. Repeat the cycle.
Benefits:
- Increases energy, reduces stress, enhances focus, and strengthens the immune system. Wim Hof's Method is also associated with improved cold tolerance.

17. Holotropic Breathwork (Stanislav Grof):
Instructions:
- Engage in deep and rhythmic breathing, often accompanied by evocative music. The goal is to induce altered states of consciousness and access deeper levels of the psyche. Holotropic Breathwork is often practiced in a group setting with a trained facilitator.
Benefits:
- Facilitates emotional release, spiritual exploration, and self-discovery. It's often used as a therapeutic tool for personal growth.

18. Circular Breathing:
Instructions:
- This technique involves continuous, connected breath without pauses between inhalation and exhalation. Breathe in through the nose and immediately exhale through the mouth in a circular, uninterrupted motion.
Benefits:
- Enhances energy flow, releases emotional blockages, and promotes a sense of connectedness. Circular breathing is used in various traditions for its meditative and transformative qualities.

19. Belly Button Healing Breath:
Instructions:
- Place one hand on the belly button and inhale deeply through the nose, expanding the abdomen. Exhale through the mouth, pushing the belly button inward. Repeat this process, focusing on the connection between the breath and the movement of the belly button.
Benefits:
- Aims to stimulate the solar plexus, improving digestion and promoting relaxation. Eastern healing practices inspire this technique.

20. Pineal Gland/Kundalini Breath:
Instructions:
- Begin with diaphragmatic breathing, focusing on the breath entering and leaving through the third eye (center of the forehead). As you breathe in, visualize energy rising from the base of the spine to the crown of the head, activating the pineal gland. Exhale, imagining the energy flowing back down.
Benefits:
- Associated with spiritual awakening, enhanced intuition, and a deeper connection to inner wisdom. This breathwork is often linked to Kundalini practices, which aim to awaken dormant spiritual energy.

These breathwork techniques offer a diverse range of benefits and experiences. As always, practice with awareness and, if necessary, consult with a healthcare professional before exploring new breathwork practices, especially if you have underlying health concerns. Remember to practice these techniques mindfully and adapt them to your comfort level. If you have health concerns, consult a healthcare professional before incorporating new breathing practices. You may have noticed that the last of the breathworks was the pineal gland/kundalini breathwork. We want to discuss Kundalini within this chapter because several master meditators bring this up in their teachings. Some people may not even take this book seriously if we did not include Kundalini. In self-discovery and spiritual awakening, Kundalini stands as a profound force, often described as the dormant serpent energy coiled at the base of the spine. Yogic traditions, including insights from luminaries like Joe Dispenza, shed light on the intricate process of awakening Kundalini energy. This chapter aims to unravel the mysteries surrounding Kundalini, exploring the physiological and metaphysical dimensions, the activation process, and the transformative benefits awaiting those who embark on this profound journey.

Kundalini:

- The term "kundalini" is derived from the Sanskrit word "kundal," which means coiled or spiraled. The idea is that this dormant spiritual energy lies coiled like a serpent at the base of the spine, specifically in the sacrum. When awakened, this energy is said to rise through the central energy channel or subtle energy pathway known as the "sushumna," which runs along the spinal column. The awakening of kundalini is considered a profound and transformative spiritual experience. It is believed to lead to higher consciousness, spiritual enlightenment, and a deep union with the divine. The process of awakening kundalini is often associated with various practices, including specific forms of yoga, meditation, breathwork, and spiritual disciplines.

The Physiology of Kundalini:

- Central to the understanding of Kundalini is its physiological manifestation, intricately linked to the body's subtle energy systems. Many yogic practitioners emphasize the sutures' role at the skull's base and the sacrum in Kundalini activation. When breathing in, the sutures open, and the sacrum flexes backward. Conversely, the sutures close during exhalation, and the sacrum flexes forward. This synchronized movement is considered an essential aspect of facilitating the flow of Kundalini energy along the spinal column.

Activating Kundalini:

- Activating Kundalini involves awakening the dormant energy, often seen as the initial stage of the transformative journey. This can be approached through various practices, including breathwork, meditation, and specific yogic postures. The emphasis here is on initiating the flow of energy, preparing the body and mind for the more profound shifts that come with the full Kundalini awakening.

Achieving Kundalini:

- Achieving Kundalini signifies the culmination of the awakening process, where the coiled energy ascends through the chakras, reaching the crown of the head. This advanced state is associated with heightened consciousness, expanded awareness, and a deep spiritual connection. Achieving Kundalini represents the harmonious integration of this powerful force into daily life.

How to Activate Kundalini:

Breathwork and Meditation:
- Engage in rhythmic and conscious breathing practices, synchronizing breath with awareness. Meditation, primarily focusing on the spine and breath, can create a conducive environment for Kundalini activation.

Chakra Alignment:
- Work on balancing and aligning the body's energy centers or chakras. Practices that focus on each chakra create a clear pathway for the upward movement of Kundalini energy.

Yogic Poses (Asanas):
- Incorporate specific yoga postures designed to stimulate the energy centers along the spine. Practices like Cobra Pose (Bhujangasana) and the Snake Pose (Sarpasana) are believed to activate Kundalini. We're going to break down these two poses for you. Keep in mind that not every yogic practitioner uses these poses, but they are common in the teachings of Kundalini. We will explain these two poses, cobra and snake before we move on to more information about Kundalini.

Cobra Pose (Bhujangasana):
- The Cobra Pose is a yoga pose that resembles the raised hood of a cobra. Here's a simple description:

Starting Position:
- Lie face-down on the yoga mat, legs extended, and hands placed beneath the shoulders.

Inhale and Lift:
- Inhale deeply as you press the palms into the mat, gently lifting the upper body. Keep the elbows slightly bent.

Arch the Back:
- As you lift, arch your back, allowing the chest to open and the shoulders to roll back. Keep the gaze forward or slightly upward.

Engage Core Muscles:
- Engage the muscles of the lower back and buttocks to support the arch in the spine.

Hold and Breathe:
- Hold the pose for a few breaths, continuing to breathe deeply. Feel the stretch in the front of the body.

Exhale and Release:
- Exhale as you slowly lower the upper body back to the mat, returning to the starting position.

Snake Pose (Sarpasana):
- The Snake Pose is another yoga pose associated with Kundalini energy. Here's a simple description:

Starting Position:
- Begin by lying on your stomach, legs extended, and forehead resting on the mat.
Place Palms:
- Position your palms next to your chest, elbows tucked close to the body.
Inhale and Lift:
- Inhale deeply, using your back muscles to lift your head, chest, and upper abdomen off the mat. Keep the lower body relaxed.
Extend Arms:
- Straighten your arms, lifting the upper body higher. Imagine creating a gentle curve in your spine, resembling a snake's upward movement.
Open the Chest:
- Allow the chest to open, and keep the shoulders relaxed away from the ears.
Hold and Breathe:
- Hold the pose, breathing smoothly. Feel the stretch in the front of the body and the activation of the back muscles.
Exhale and Lower:
- Slowly exhale as you lower the upper body, resting the forehead on the mat.

Remember, it's essential to practice these poses with awareness, honoring your body's limitations, and seeking guidance from a qualified yoga instructor if you're new to these poses or have any health concerns.

Benefits of Kundalini Activation and Achievement:

Heightened Awareness:
- Kundalini's awakening brings an increased self-awareness, enabling individuals to perceive their thoughts, emotions, and experiences with greater clarity.
Spiritual Connection:
- Achieving Kundalini fosters a profound connection to the spiritual dimension, allowing individuals to tap into a higher consciousness and sense of universal unity.

Emotional Release:
- Kundalini activation facilitates the release of stored emotional energy, leading to emotional healing and a more balanced emotional state.
Enhanced Creativity:
- Many practitioners report heightened creativity and a deeper connection to inspiration after Kundalini awakening.
Physical Vitality:
- The flow of Kundalini energy is believed to invigorate the physical body, promoting vitality and overall well-being.
Conclusion:
- Embarking on the journey of Kundalini is a transformative venture that transcends the physical and the metaphysical boundaries. Whether one seeks to activate or achieve Kundalini, the path unfolds as a profound exploration of the self and a reconnection to the vast and limitless realms of consciousness. As with any spiritual journey, patience, dedication, and respect for the process are vital companions on this enlightening expedition.

We want to wrap up this chapter by helping you set your intentions and devise a plan before you meditate each time. What would you like to achieve during this meditation? How could you try to accomplish this goal? How long can you dedicate to this meditation? The last thing you want is to feel rushed during a meditation. So please think these things through beforehand to get better results.

Setting the Stage:
- Before delving into the following meditation, lay the foundation for your transformative experience. Clarify the potential you wish to unlock and draw towards you. As you prepare, remember that all possibilities already reside in the quantum field, awaiting your conscious awareness and resonance.

Symbolizing Your Desire:
- Identify the experience you crave, assigning it a capital letter as a symbolic representation. Envision two squiggly circular lines around the letter, embodying your brain's electrical field of thought and the magnetic field of feeling from your heart. These fields will align with the potential in the quantum, forming the bridge to your desired reality. For instance, choose "L" to symbolize your aspiration for love.

Defining Your Vision:
- Explain your intention by listing specific conditions for your envisioned reality. This step adds depth and clarity to your intention. Avoid stipulating a timeframe, allowing the quantum to orchestrate the perfect synchronicity. Craft conditions like owning your own company, collaborating with brilliance, making a global impact, embracing remote work, and being a perpetual traveler.

Igniting Heart-Centered Emotions:
- Envision the emotional landscape that will accompany the manifestation of your desired reality. Create a list of elevated emotions, understanding that these heart-centered energies will propel your intent into manifestation. Begin with the potent emotion of gratitude, a magnetic force that aligns with the receiving of abundance.

Elevated Emotions Playlist:
- Compose a symphony of emotions that will accompany realizing your dream job. Feel empowered, unlimited, grateful, free, in awe, in love with life, worthy, and joyful. Each emotion acts as a note in the composition of your quantum symphony, resonating with the frequencies of your desired reality.

Manifestation Unleashed:
- Witness the alchemy of intention and emotion as you prepare to tune into the quantum symphony of your best self. Your intentions, symbolized by a letter, are charged with the electricity of thought and the magnetism of feeling, creating a harmonious bridge to the quantum field. Define your vision, embrace heart-centered emotions, and orchestrate a transformative journey toward manifesting your dreams. You are the conductor of your quantum symphony, and the universe eagerly awaits the notes you choose to play.

Before we move beyond meditation and other topics, we want to mention a simple exercise we recommend for anyone who has not meditated, has yet to meditate much, or is having trouble with meditation. This is a quick and easy practice meditation, and it can just be for sixty seconds. First, close your eyes and take a deep breath. Slow your breathing down as much as you can; deep breaths in and deep breaths out nice and slow. Now, place one or both hands on your chest and feel your heartbeat. Place your focus on your heart and your lungs as you breathe in and out. As a little bonus to this exercise, you can fake a smile while breathing and focusing on your heart. Even a fake smile releases endorphins, so the counterfeit smile quickly becomes genuine. And that's the exercise.

Could you try it for sixty seconds? You will feel at least somewhat better no matter how bad you feel at the time. Try taking your hand(s) off your chest and still try to sense your heart. You can also try this exercise with your eyes open. You can get the same results from this meditation with your eyes open and without your hand(s) on your chest. So when you get skilled at sensing your heart with your eyes closed and your hand on your heart, try to get adept at sensing it without touch and with the added distraction of sight. This practice can eventually become something you do throughout the day, just for a few seconds or for however long it takes for its effects to set in. Your heart is your elevated emotions energy center, so use it. Learn to get comfortable sensing and allowing it to fill your body with high emotions. Those elevated emotions will fill your mind with elevated thoughts. Positive emotions combined with positive thoughts will lead to positive actions.

CHAPTER 9: FREQUENCY

We mentioned before how much frequencies play a role in meditations. That's because we are energy, and energy has a vibrational frequency. Our energy affects other energies around us and vice versa. So, listening to specific frequencies can do wonders for your mind and body. There have been countless studies on frequencies and their effects. Luckily, we can search them out now instead of figuring out which ones are best. Science has discovered different effects each frequency has on our mind and body, and we can benefit from their research and use different frequencies to accomplish other goals. Studies have even proven that when you play specific frequencies and tracks to plants, they grow faster and more robust than usual due to the constant stream of positive frequencies you've played in their direction. This kind of research found that classical music also helps plants grow. There's even a device that can help us hear the frequency of a specific plant vibrating. The device has a speaker and two small clamps, as seen on a voltmeter. Attaching these clamps to any living plant measures the frequency at which water travels through the plant. It turns that information into music that plays through the speaker. If plants can benefit from frequencies, then we absolutely can benefit from frequencies as well. This chart shows us which specific frequencies benefit each energy center. Below this diagram we will introduce you to several expected meditation and relaxation track frequencies and list their benefits.

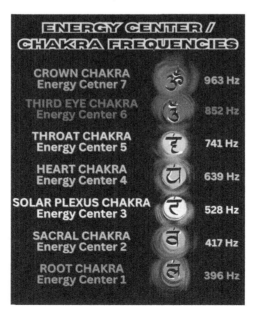

ENERGY CENTER / CHAKRA FREQUENCIES

CROWN CHAKRA Energy Cetner 7	ॐ	963 Hz
THIRD EYE CHAKRA Energy Center 6	३	852 Hz
THROAT CHAKRA Energy Center 5	हं	741 Hz
HEART CHAKRA Energy Center 4	व	639 Hz
SOLAR PLEXUS CHAKRA Energy Center 3	र	528 Hz
SACRAL CHAKRA Energy Center 2	व	417 Hz
ROOT CHAKRA Energy Center 1	ल	396 Hz

396 Hz - Liberating Guilt and Fear:
- Listening to this frequency is thought to help release guilt and fear, promoting a sense of liberation and inner peace.

417 Hz - Undoing Situations and Facilitating Change:
- At 417 Hz, the music aims to assist in undoing challenging situations, fostering change, and promoting positive transformations. It is believed to transmute pain and trauma as well as facilitate healing and release of traumatic experiences.

528 Hz - Love Frequency:
- Recognized as the Love Frequency, 528 Hz enhances the harmonious vibrations associated with love, healing, and inner peace.

639 Hz - Connecting and Relationships:
- This frequency is associated with improving connections and relationships and fostering understanding, communication, and harmony.

741 Hz - Expression and Solutions:
- Tuned to 741 Hz, music is thought to support self-expression and finding solutions to problems, promoting empowerment. It is also related to cleansing and detoxification.

852 Hz - Awakening Intuition:
- Frequencies at 852 Hz stimulate and awaken intuition, enhancing spiritual awareness and inner guidance. Thought to help align with the spiritual order of the universe.

963 Hz - Pineal Gland Activation:
- Associated with the activation of the pineal gland, listening to 963 Hz frequencies facilitates higher states of consciousness and spiritual awakening.

Other Beneficial Frequencies:

174 Hz - Pain Relief:
- Often associated with pain reduction and releasing physical and emotional pain.

285 Hz - Healing and Revitalization:
- Linked to the body's energy field for enhanced healing.

*432 Hz - Previous Standard Tuning for Music:
- Sense of harmony with nature, emotional resonance, spiritual connection, and improved sleep.

444 Hz - Transformation and Miracles:
- Believed to be a frequency associated with transformation and the manifestation of miracles.

888 Hz – Divine Abundance:
- Thought to resonate with the energy of abundance and align with divine forces
936 Hz – Pineal Gland Activation:
- Similar to 963 Hz, it's linked to the activation of the pineal gland and spiritual development

There are plenty of other positive frequencies; these are just some commonly used frequencies. The energy centers themselves aren't measured in frequency, but in sound healing and vibrational medicine, practitioners suggest that exposing the body to specific frequencies through sound or music can have therapeutic effects on each energy center. For example, if you're looking to liberate guilt and fear stored in your root chakra/1st energy center, then listen to a 369 frequency. A side note about these frequencies is that there are also frequencies that negatively affect us. We don't see the need to make a long list of those frequencies, but one in particular affects us all. 440 Hz became the new music tuning standard in the early 20th century. The decision to standardize pitch at 440 Hz from 432 Hz was made during the International Conference on Weights and Measures in 1939. However, the adoption of this standard occurred gradually, and it wasn't universally accepted until later. Now, this book isn't about conspiracies, and we're not going to go on a tangent about the people in charge who control society but ask yourself why the people in charge may have wanted to change the standard of tuning for music. You can find countless videos of people showing the difference between 432 Hz and 440 Hz online. It's quite a difference in the sound, and you can even notice how your body and mind react to the two different frequencies; it's not exactly subtle. Look at the difference!

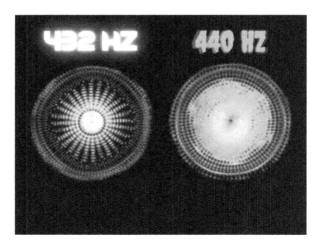

Now, we also want to explain brain frequencies. These frequencies are measured differently than body frequencies because they measure the frequencies at which our brain neurons release energy. So, if you're wondering why brain frequencies are between 0-140 Hz instead of 852-963 Hz, as we show in the energy centers chart, know that it's essentially like comparing apples to oranges. They're two different kinds of frequencies. So, let's unravel the nuances of the five key brainwave frequencies, offering insights into their functions and how you can harness them for personal growth and well-being.

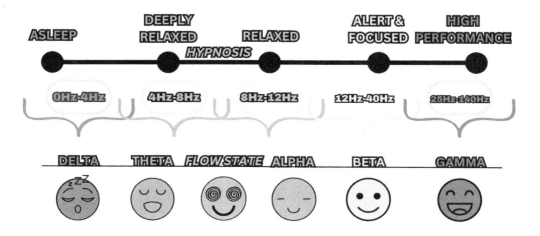

Delta Waves: The Deep Restorers:

- Delta waves, the slowest brainwaves, guide you into deep relaxation and restorative sleep. Think of "Delta" for "Deep." Associated with unconscious bodily functions, they regulate the cardiovascular and digestive systems. While healthy levels contribute to restful sleep, irregular delta wave activity may link to learning difficulties or awareness issues.

- **Frequency Range:** 0 Hz to 4 Hz
- **High Levels:** Brain injuries, severe ADHD
- **Low Levels:** Poor sleep, inability to rejuvenate
- **Optimal Range:** Healthy immune system, restorative REM sleep

Theta Waves: The Gateway to Creativity:

- Theta waves, the 'suggestible waves,' thrive during daydreaming, sleep, and hypnotic states. Known for inducing a relaxed, open mind, excess theta activity may lead to bouts of depression. Yet, theta brings benefits, enhancing creativity and intuition and fostering emotional connections.

- **Frequency Range:** 4 Hz to 8 Hz
- **High Levels:** ADHD, depressive states
- **Low Levels:** Anxiety, poor emotional awareness
- **Optimal Range:** Maximum creativity, deep emotional connection, more excellent intuition

Flow State: The Harmonious Symphony:

- Flow state, often called "in the zone," is characterized by intense focus, heightened creativity, and optimal performance. In the optimal flow state, theta and alpha waves work synergistically, allowing the mind to enter a relaxed yet highly focused state. Theta waves contribute to creative thinking, while alpha waves maintain a calm and focused mental environment. This delicate interplay results in heightened performance and a profound sense of fulfillment.

- **Flow State Frequency:** Vary but is often associated with the mid-range of theta and alpha waves, typically around 8 Hz to 14 Hz.
- **High Levels in Flow State:** Enhanced creativity, deep intuitive insights, sustained focus, and efficient task execution.
- **Low Levels in Flow State:** Potential for distraction, difficulty accessing creative flow, lack of mental clarity.
- **Optimal Range in Flow State:** Seamless integration of ideas, heightened problem-solving, calm yet alert mental state, optimal task engagement.

Alpha Waves: The Bridge of Relaxation:
- Alpha waves bridge conscious (beta) and subconscious (theta) mindsets, promoting calmness and relaxation. They are ideal for stress reduction and counterbalance excessive beta activity during heightened cognitive arousal.

- **Frequency Range:** 8 Hz to 12 Hz
- **High Levels:** Over-relaxed state, inability to focus
- **Low Levels:** OCD, anxiety symptoms
- **Optimal Range:** Ideal relaxation

Beta Waves: The Active Achievers:
- Beta waves, prevalent in wakefulness, accompany cognitive activities like reasoning and reading. While beneficial for focus and problem-solving, excessive Beta activity can lead to stress and anxiety. Consider beta as the "get things done" state of mind and high beta waves as our survival instincts of fight/flight.

- **Frequency Range:** 12 Hz to 40 Hz
- **High Levels:** Anxiety, high adrenaline levels
- **Low Levels:** Depression, lack of attention
- **Optimal Range:** Consistent focus, strong memory recall, high problem-solving ability

Gamma Waves: The Cognitive Maestros:
- A recent discovery is that gamma waves contribute to complex task processing, learning, and memory. Their optimal levels bind senses to process new information. Linked to meditation, gamma waves play a role in heightened states of being and completeness.

- **Frequency Range:** 40 Hz to 100 Hz
- **High Levels:** Anxiety, stress
- **Low Levels:** Depression, ADHD
- **Optimal Range:** Information processing, cognition, learning, binding of senses

As you navigate the realm of brain frequencies, consider each wave a tool in your mental toolkit. Mastering the orchestration of these frequencies can empower you to lead a more balanced, creative, and focused life. Explore the symphony within your brain, and let the harmonies guide you towards personal growth and well-being. What needs to be fully explained in this brainwave frequencies chart is how high beta waves are what we feel when we are stressed. This is our fight/flight response. Adrenaline courses through our body and brain, and we vibrate at high beta-brain wave frequencies. When we live a life full of stress, we experience high beta brain wave frequencies quite often, and this can begin to feel like a rather natural state when, in fact, it's only meant to be used for survival situations. The other thing that needs to be explained in this chart is that the way to get to gamma waves is through the flow or hypnosis states. You can tap into gamma waves when you meditate and become calm enough to enter that flow state/hypnosis state. You will jump up the brain wave frequencies from flow state to gamma state, surpassing alpha and beta waves. This is because being in a flow or hypnosis state causes brain coherence. Brain coherence is what happens when your brain is essentially in sync. The brain waves are no longer messy and incoherent. They align with each other, and your thought patterns become more apparent. Brain coherence also allows all parts of the brain to communicate better. Right and left hemispheres, frontal lobe, midbrain, and the inner brain. Let's break this down for you.

Stress and High Beta Waves:
The brainwave frequencies chart provides valuable insight into our mental states. Still, it needs to delve into the impact of sustained stress on our brain waves. High beta waves, typically associated with stress, represent our primal fight-or-flight response. When we encounter stressors, adrenaline surges through our bodies, causing our brains to vibrate at high beta frequencies. In the modern world, however, chronic stress has become commonplace, and high beta frequencies can feel like a default state. It's crucial to recognize that these frequencies are evolutionarily designed for survival situations and are not meant to be a constant in our daily lives. Prolonged exposure to high beta waves can have detrimental effects on both mental and physical well-being.

Flow State, Hypnosis, and Gamma Waves:
The brainwave chart highlights states like alpha and beta but doesn't explicitly explain the journey to gamma waves. Achieving gamma waves involves reaching a state of heightened awareness and mental clarity. Two paths that lead to gamma waves are the flow state and hypnosis.

Flow State:
- The flow state, often described as "in the zone," occurs when you're fully immersed in an activity. This could be anything from creative work to sports. During a flow state, the brain experiences coherence, where all brainwave frequencies align harmoniously. This coherence allows for enhanced focus, creativity, and timelessness.

Hypnosis State:
- Hypnosis, another avenue to gamma waves, involves deep relaxation and heightened suggestibility. In this state, the brain achieves a profound level of coherence, leading to increased connectivity between different brain regions. This synchronization facilitates deep mental states, making it possible to access gamma frequencies.

Brain Coherence:
- Brain coherence is where the various brainwave frequencies synchronize and align, fostering clear thought patterns and improved communication between different brain parts.

Benefits:
- Enhanced cognitive abilities, improved focus, creativity, and heightened states of awareness are among the benefits of brain coherence.

Communication between Brain Regions:
- Coherence facilitates better communication between the right and left hemispheres, frontal lobe, midbrain, and inner brain, fostering a holistic and integrated cognitive experience.

Understanding these nuances provides a more comprehensive view of how our mental states and well-being are intricately tied to our brains' frequencies, emphasizing the importance of managing stress and cultivating coherent states for optimal mental functioning. There is one other significant kind of frequency to understand: the frequency contained within essential oils. Below is an extended list with additional essential oils, noting that frequency values are approximations and can vary. Also, each essential oil brand may have different applications and usage recommendations. We're not doctors; we just want to explain the frequencies, benefits, and applications/usages of some of the most popular essential oils.

Essential Oils Frequencies:

Idaho Blue Spruce: The Forest's Wisdom
- **Frequency:** ~580 MHz
- **Benefits:** Grounding, respiratory support.
- **Usage:** Inhale or diffuse to evoke the essence of the outdoors.

Rose Oil: The Heart's Embrace
- **Frequency:** ~320 MHz
- **Benefits:** Emotional balance, skin rejuvenation.
- **Usage:** Apply to pulse points or dilute and use in skincare routines.

Ylang Ylang: The Sensual Harmonizer
- **Frequency:** ~150 MHz
- **Benefits:** Aphrodisiac, mood enhancement.
- **Usage:** Apply to pulse points or diffuse.

Frankincense: The Meditative Essence
- **Frequency:** ~147 MHz
- **Benefits:** Meditation, immune support.
- **Usage:** Apply to wrists or diffuse during meditation.

Lavender: The Relaxation Elixir
- **Frequency:** ~118 MHz
- **Benefits:** Calming, relaxation, sleep support.
- **Usage:** Apply to temples or diffuse in the bedroom.

Clary Sage: The Hormonal Harmonizer
- **Frequency:** ~105 MHz
- **Benefits:** Hormonal balance, relaxation.
- **Usage:** Apply or diffuse.

Neroli: The Calming Citrus
- **Frequency:** ~105 MHz
- **Benefits:** Calming, skincare.
- **Usage:** Apply or diffuse.

Myrrh: The Spiritual Connector
- **Frequency:** ~105 MHz
- **Benefits:** Meditation, spiritual connection.
- **Usage:** Apply or diffuse during introspective practices.

Chamomile: The Serene Soother
- **Frequency:** ~105 MHz
- **Benefits:** Calming, sleep support.
- **Usage:** Dilute and apply or diffuse before bedtime.

Juniper Berry: The Purifying Essence
- **Frequency:** ~98 MHz
- **Benefits:** Purification, grounding.
- **Usage:** Apply topically or diffusely.

Sandalwood: The Meditative Essence
- **Frequency:** ~96 MHz
- **Benefits:** Meditation, calming.
- **Usage:** Apply or diffuse during meditation.

White Angelica: The Protective Veil
- **Frequency:** ~89 MHz
- **Benefits:** Emotional protection, energy clearing.
- **Usage:** Apply to shoulders, wrists, or diffuse to create an energetic shield.

Peppermint: The Energizing Mint
- **Frequency:** ~78 MHz
- **Benefits:** Energizing, digestion support.
- **Usage:** Inhale or apply to the back of the neck.

Jasmine: The Mood Elevation Elixir
- **Frequency:** ~75 MHz
- **Benefits:** Mood enhancement, skin support.
- **Usage:** Apply to pulse points or diffuse.

Lemon: The Uplifting Citrus
- **Frequency:** ~75 MHz
- **Benefits:** Uplifting, mood enhancement.
- **Usage:** Diffuse or add to water.

Bergamot: The Uplifting Citrus
- **Frequency:** ~74 MHz
- **Benefits:** Uplifting, stress relief.
- **Usage:** Diffuse or apply to pulse points.

Lemongrass: The Zesty Energizer
- **Frequency:** ~72 MHz
- **Benefits:** Energizing, insect repellent.
- **Usage:** Diffuse or apply diluted to skin.

Eucalyptus: The Respiratory Revitalizer
- **Frequency:** ~66 MHz
- **Benefits:** Respiratory support, invigorating.
- **Usage:** Inhale or diffuse during cold seasons.

Rosemary: The Clarity Companion
- **Frequency:** ~66 MHz
- **Benefits:** Mental clarity, memory support.
- **Usage:** Diffuse while studying or working.

Patchouli: The Earthy Calm
- **Frequency:** ~58 MHz
- **Benefits:** Grounding, calming.
- **Usage:** Apply or diffuse.

Geranium: The Emotional Alchemist
- **Frequency:** ~52 MHz
- **Benefits:** Emotional balance, skin care.
- **Usage:** Apply topically or diffusely.

Cedarwood: The Grounding Guardian
- **Frequency:** ~50 MHz
- **Benefits:** Grounding, emotional balance.
- **Usage:** Apply to wrists or diffuse.

Tea Tree (Melaleuca): The Cleansing Protector
- **Frequency:** ~48 MHz
- **Benefits:** Antiseptic, skin support.
- **Usage:** Apply topically to skin irritations.

CHAPTER 10: SELF-AWARENESS

Self-awareness is recognizing and understanding one's emotions, strengths, weaknesses, values, and motivations. It involves introspection and an accurate assessment of oneself. Identifying our programs/patterns is how we develop self-awareness. Choosing not to repeat the cycle is growth. Repeating the cycle can lead to a miserable life. What makes people stuck in misery? They become accustomed to it, it becomes their norm, and they become addicted to the stress that their mind and body have become used to inducing. The patterns become so repetitive that it begins to feel comfortable to the miserable person. It then becomes more difficult for them to change than to stay in misery because of their comfort in their bad habits. Change only happens when it's easier to change than to stay the same. This is often why it takes a rock bottom for people to change. They finally recognize that their life has become so miserable that they now see changing to be easier than staying the same. So what's the difference in the scenario where the bad habits are the same, but the person feels it's easier to change vs. harder to change? Awareness. Once you become aware of the reasons that your limiting beliefs and bad habits are being held onto, you can begin logically deconstructing why you're allowing these habits and beliefs to rule your own life. You will cut off your hand before cutting off your arm every time. If you want to be successful, but deep down you're afraid of putting yourself out there and being judged, then you will cut off the hand (not be successful) as opposed to going against your belief of being afraid to put yourself out there to be judged (cutting off your arm). So you see, we choose the most comfortable choice every time. We can succeed once we overcome that fear of judgment, failure, etc.

The same goes for bad habits like smoking cigarettes or drinking alcohol. If we can begin unraveling the reasons we enjoy doing these things and see that there are falsehoods within some of those lies we tell ourselves, we can begin seeing that it would be easier to quit this bad habit than to keep doing it. For the smoking cigarettes example, many believe that it is a stress relief to smoke. When we realize that cigarettes are what is causing the stress to begin with, we can realize that it's not actually a stress relief. It's actually a stress loop. We feel stress when our body doesn't have enough nicotine in our system, so we smoke not to feel that stress, but the nicotine is what caused the stress in the first place. We continue to cut off the hand (smoke another cigarette) instead of cutting off the arm (quitting the habit, feeling withdrawals, and having to find another way to cope with stress). When we're able to see that going through the withdrawal period for a short time would be less stressful than continuously living in this stress loop, it then becomes easier to change and quit the habit.

Our bodies work with our minds to produce hormones to help us feel what we are thinking. When we get stuck in a negative loop, our bodies understand that we need stress hormones to achieve normalcy. So what is usually a beneficial attribute of the body now becomes what keeps us stuck feeling negative. You may notice some patterns within your stress as well. If you drive to work in the morning and feel stressed about traffic every day, then on the days that you don't work, your body may start creating stress hormones at the same time even though you're not in traffic. The body knows, "Oh, it's that time; we're supposed to feel stress right now, so let's help feel stress. Release the stress hormones!" We have to step out of the loop and recognize what the body is doing and what the mind is doing.

Become the observer instead of feeling trapped as the ego so we can see what's going on and decide what we want to change. We hold ourselves back with our fears and our beliefs. The best way to get good at something is to start doing it. It sounds simple but will hold us back until we flip the switch and change gears. We must expand our mindset and our perspective. We then put on a new lens to see the world. No more dark aviators to cloud our worldview or our reality. Every situation can be handled with positivity or negativity, including problems where negativity is thrown at you.

Try seeing all of your thoughts and feelings objectively. Understand that our subconscious is trying to talk to us through emotions. So when we feel uncomfortable, it's the unconscious expressing something to us. What is it? Well, it starts as a feeling in the body. Energy is being trapped somewhere specific. It's usually one of the bottom three energy centers because that's where we carry most negative energy. Based on its location, our mind already knows what that emotion is. It begins communicating that emotion through the voice in our head. Some of us are better at hearing the voice than others. And some of us, through practice, have been able to stay present and recognize our voice any time it begins speaking. That voice is our mind decoding the emotion of the subconscious through the feelings it sends to the body. The third chakra is where we hold our self-esteem, and the second is where we have our power and creativity. The first chakra is where we hold our sense of safety and security. Energy can become caught in other centers of the body. Still, most negative emotions are stored in these lower three centers.

A tool that may help is the Emotion Code Chart. Bradley Nelson created it, and it may help you better indicate which emotions are stuck in your body based on their location. Let's explain how to read and use The Emotion Code Chart. Look at the Emotions Code Chart, which lists various emotions. Identify the feelings you suspect might be trapped within you or someone else. Use muscle testing (applied kinesiology) to determine if a specific emotion is present. This involves applying gentle pressure to a muscle while focusing on the suspected emotion. If the muscle weakens, it might indicate the presence of that emotion. Column A often contains broader emotion categories or themes. These can include general emotions like Anger, Sadness, Fear, or more specific emotional themes. For example, under the theme of "Abandonment," you might find particular emotions related to feeling abandoned. Column B lists specific emotions falling under the broader categories in Column A. These are more detailed and nuanced emotions. For instance, if Column A is "Grief," Column B might include specific emotions like "Heartbroken" or "Deep Sorrow."

Emotion Code Chart:

Row 1 Heart Or Small Intestine:
- **Column A:** Abandonment, Betrayal, Forlorn, Lost, Love Unreceived.
- Column B: Effort Unreceived, Heartache, Insecurity, Overjoy, Vulnerability.

Row 2 Spleen Or Stomach:
- **Column A:** Anxiety, Despair, Disgust, Nervousness, Worry.
- **Column B:** Failure, Helplessness, Hopelessness, Lack Of Control, Low Self-Esteem.

Row 3 Lung Or Colon:
- **Column A:** Crying, Discouragement, Rejection, Sadness, Sorrow.
- **Column B:** Confusion, Defensiveness, Grief, Self-Abuse, Stubbornness.

Row 4 Liver Or Gallbladder:
- **Column A:** Anger, Bitterness, Guilt, Hatred, Resentment.
- **Column B:** Depression, Frustration, Indecisiveness, Panic, Taken For Granted.

Row 5 Kidneys Or Bladder:
- **Column A:** Blaming, Dread, Fear, Horror, Peeved.
- **Column B:** Conflict, Creative Insecurity, Terror, Unsupported, Wishy Washy.

Row 6 Glands Or Sexual Organs:
- Column A: Humiliation, Jealousy, Longing, Lust, Overwhelm.
- Column B: Pride, Shame, Shock, Unworthy, Worthlessness.

Other Possible Emotion Codes:

Chest: fear **Stomach:** intuition **Full body:** happiness
Head: anger **Muscles:** anxiety **Face:** shame
Mouth: disgust **Throat:** sadness **Jaw:** frustration
Shoulders: burden **Neck:** stress **Hips:** suppressed trauma
Thumb: worry **Index finger:** fear **Middle finger:** anger
Ring finger: sorrow **Pinky finger:** low self-esteem

Another tool that may help us understand what emotions are causing us physical ailments is the meridian system. The meridian system is a concept central to traditional Chinese medicine (TCM), including practices like acupuncture and Reiki. It involves energy pathways, known as meridians, that flow throughout the body, carrying vital energy or life force, often referred to as "Qi" or "Chi."

Here's an overview: "Qi" and "Chi" refer to the same concept but are spelled differently based on the system of Romanization used. Both terms are used to represent the vital life force or energy in traditional Chinese philosophy, particularly in practices like traditional Chinese medicine, Qigong, and martial arts.

"Qi" is the Pinyin romanization of the Chinese word 气, which translates to "air," "breath," or "energy." Pinyin is the official system of Romanization for Standard Mandarin Chinese.

"Chi" is an alternative romanization, often used in Western literature, following a different system called Wade-Giles. The term "Chi" is an older transliteration that predates Pinyin but is still familiar to many people.

In essence, whether you see "Qi" or "Chi," they both represent the same fundamental concept of the vital energy or life force believed to flow through the body and the universe in traditional Chinese thought. The choice between "Qi" and "Chi" is more a matter of the Romanization system used rather than a difference in meaning.

Here is a diagram that shows the meridian system:

THE MERIDIAN SYSTEM

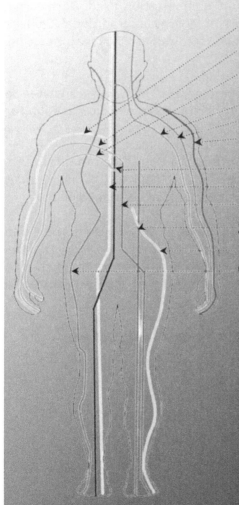

Lung Meridian
Pericardium Meridian
Heart Meridian

Colon Meridian
Triple Warmer Meridian
Intestine Meridian

Urinary Bladder Meridian
Stomach Meridian
Liver Meridian

Spleen Meridian
Kidney Meridian
Gall Bladder Meridian

Meridians:
- TCM has 12 primary meridians, each associated with specific organs and organ systems.
- These meridians are channels through which energy flows, connecting the body's surface with its internal organs.
- Each meridian has specific points where it can be accessed for therapeutic purposes.

Acupuncture Points:
- Acupuncture is a TCM practice involving inserting thin needles into specific points along the meridians.
- These acupuncture points are believed to correspond to areas where energy flow can be influenced or balanced.
- The goal is to promote the free flow of Qi, addressing imbalances and promoting overall well-being.

Reiki and Energy Healing:
- Although originating in Japan, Reiki shares some concepts with TCM, including working with energy.
- In Reiki, practitioners use their hands to channel energy into the recipient, aiming to balance and harmonize the body's energy.
- While Reiki doesn't focus on meridians in the same way as acupuncture, it shares the overarching idea of working with the body's energy systems.

Energy Flow and Balance:
- The meridian system is based on the principle that good health is maintained when the flow of Qi is balanced and unobstructed.
- Imbalances or blockages in the meridians are thought to contribute to various physical and mental health issues.
- Practices like acupuncture and Reiki aim to restore balance by influencing energy flow.

It's important to note that while these concepts are deeply ingrained in traditional healing practices, the meridian system and the existence of Qi are not universally accepted within the framework of Western medicine. Research on the effectiveness of acupuncture and energy healing is ongoing, and individual experiences with these practices can vary. But we can learn from these techniques and use them to help us better understand our body, what's going on within it, and how to better regulate our energy flow within.

Lastly, we will include our chart for Unbalanced Chakra Symptoms. Between these three references, you should know what's happening with your body, emotions, and energy centers/chakras. If you are experiencing pain, blockages, or discomfort, look at these three references to help understand which emotion and energy center it correlates with. If you notice a particular mental state or feeling within yourself, look at these three references to help understand which energy center may be blocked, what emotions relate to that mental state, or which mental state relates to your feeling.

UNBALANCED CHAKRA SYMPTOMS

	Overactive Personality	Physical Ailments	Underactive Personality
	Addicted To Spirituality, Careless Of Bodily Needs, Difficulty Controlling Emotions	Dizziness, Confusion, Mental Fog, Neurological Disorders, Nerve Pain, Mental Disorders	Cynicism, Dispregarding What Is Sacred, Unable to Set Or Maintain Goals, Lacking Direction
	Lacking Good Judgement, Out Of Touch With Reality, Unable To Focus, Hallucinating	Vision Problems, Headaches, Migraines, Sleeping Disorders, Seizures, Nightmares	Lack Of Direction, Lack Of Clarity, Ridgid Thinking, Fearful Of Future, Cling To the Past, Distrustful, Reliant On Authority
	Loud, Overly Talkative, Unable To Listen, Highly Critical, Verbally Abusive, Condescending	Stiff/Sore Neck Or Shoulders, Sore Throat, Hoarseness, Thyroid Issues	Quiet, Shy, Difficulty Speaking Your Truth, Introverted, Withdrawn
	Letting Everyone In, Clingy, Suffocating, Lack Of Sense Of Self In Relationships, Lacking Boundaries,	Poor Circulation, High Blood Pressure, Ashtma, Heart Attacks, Breast Cancer, Stiff Joints	Depressed, Distant, Grudgeful, Lack Of Discipline, Unwilling To Open Up With Others
	Control Issues, Domineering, Aggressiveness, Anger, Perfectionism, Overly Critical, Manipulative	Ulcers, Gas, Nausea, Digestive Problems, Eating Disorders, Liver Or Kidney Infection	Passive, Indecisive, Timid, Lacking Self Control, Easily Controlled
	Overly Emotional, Attachment To Others, Dramatic, Moody, Lack Boundaries, Hypersexual	Lower Back Pain, Uniary Issues, Kidney Pain, Infertility, Impotence	Low Self-Esteem, Lack Of Creativity, Unemotional, Impotence, Closed Off, Low Sex Drive
	Fear Of Abandonment, Nervousness, Insecurity, Greedy, Materialistic, Ungrounded, Codependent, Fearfulness,	Restless, Unhealthy Weight, Constipation, Cramps, Heavy Menstrual, Fatigue	Fear Of Abandonment, Nervousness, Insecurity, Greedy, Materialistic, Ungrounded, Codependent, Fearfulness,

Where that energy gets trapped tells us what our subconscious tries to communicate. If you're aware of the emotional symptom but unsure how to help alleviate it, find that symptom in the chart and see which energy center it is related to. Play frequencies that help with that center, do meditations that focus on that center or perhaps use the meridian system to help alleviate those issues. If you're aware of the physical symptom but unsure of what is causing it, then find that energy center on the chart and see what emotions may be causing you to feel pain or discomfort in that center. Find frequencies, meditations, or other helpful tools to alleviate the symptoms. The mind will generally be able to translate this for us as well. So, for instance, if you're feeling unmotivated, then there may be a root issue underneath that's causing you to feel uncomfortable and not motivated, but your mind does decode it by nagging at you about your problems it has decided are worth you paying attention to. If those same thoughts and feelings keep occurring in our daily lives, then notice it as a message or a lesson for you to learn or decode from your subconscious that is being communicated through your body to get your attention.

While becoming more self-aware, the goal is to stay focused on what your mind and body tell you throughout the day. It will be hard always to stay aware, but you'll quickly build up to that. The more effort you put in, the quicker you learn the skill. You most likely won't be able to stay aware at all times, but the most crucial time to be aware is when you feel negative emotions or hear negative thoughts. Some thoughts you may not even realize are negative unless you're paying attention to them and what they're causing the body to do in response. Thinking and feeling work in tandem, so if you notice one, the other will also be present. If you notice the thought, look for the feeling it creates. And if you notice the feeling, try to hear what the thought is saying, and instead of just listening to it and letting it control you, decide to tune it out because you know it's lying to you if it's making you feel negative. The next step would be to investigate it once you have control, no longer letting it sink you into constant negative energy. Once you have discovered what's keeping that negativity inside you, you can begin forgiving and letting it all go.

CHAPTER 11: MINDFULNESS

We have arrived at the 3rd M! Arguably, the most important of the Ms. Mindfulness is an extension of self-awareness. Once we become self-aware, we can become more curious about what's happening inside and better diagnose our internal issues and traumas. Mindfulness is a state of non-judgmental awareness of the present moment. It involves paying attention to thoughts and feelings without getting entangled in them. Mindfulness practices, such as meditation, aim to cultivate this state, fostering clarity, focus, and a sense of calm. Becoming self-aware is the first step. Now that you're more self-aware, the next step is recognizing and challenging your patterns with mindfulness. So how do we achieve this?

Once we have become aware of ourselves and how our mind and body respond to the exterior world, we can change those habits, attitudes, programs, and beliefs one step at a time. Picture your thoughts like a ticker scrolling by, as you see at the bottom of sports, news, or stock broadcasts. There are so many scrolling by at all times that we eventually latch on to one. Most of the time, we let the outside world affect which of these we latch on to. We'll use the example of somebody saying something mean to us. Then, right away, all the thoughts related to people being mean to us come into our awareness. "You suck," "You are a failure," "You can't do that," and if we feel like those thoughts are true, then we'll give in to them. We'll start spiraling and thinking about all the things surrounding those negative feelings we have about ourselves. But if we don't relate to those thoughts and know they're not true, they don't hold any weight, and we let them pass by on the ticker. Presence and mindfulness aren't about clearing our minds; they're about paying attention to our thoughts and feelings as they happen. We are not letting our autopilots go unnoticed and acknowledging everything within us instead of ignoring or abusing it. This brings out our authenticity. And being authentic is a breath of fresh air for ourselves and everyone around us.

This happens in stand-up comedy constantly. The comedian jokes about something that doesn't pertain to you and doesn't hit any nerves, so it doesn't offend you. Then, they bring up a topic that relates to you and make fun of it. Now, all of a sudden, you're triggered and hurt, and you don't think it's funny at all. Well, what's the difference? Other people are laughing at that joke you don't find funny. The difference is that you let their words bring up negative feelings and negative thoughts in your mind. If you didn't believe in their words, you wouldn't pay any kind to them. You either don't relate to the comedy and aren't affected by it, you do relate and are sensitive to the topic, or you do relate and don't let it bother you because that topic doesn't illicit negative thoughts and emotions within you anymore. Most people are stuck in the second of these three options, which brings about "cancel culture" and "outrage culture." Victim mindsets fuel these things and are not healthy for society in general.

So, let's say someone calls you an idiot. Well, if you don't believe you're an idiot, then you can laugh at that. Even if you know they weren't joking about it. You may not appreciate their attempt at upsetting you, but you won't let it hurt you because you know what they said about you wasn't true. However, if you do feel like you may be an idiot in some way, then you may end up taking offense to their words. Lastly, if you do feel like an idiot and either don't feel like they're trying to insult you or you've gained control over your emotions enough to recognize that just because you have a thought or a feeling doesn't mean you have to keep paying attention to it or feel that it's true. So you're either thinking, "Well, I'm not an idiot, so that doesn't affect me," "I am an idiot, and I feel like you are trying to hurt me, so I'm upset" or "I'm an idiot, and I'm happy to be me, so nothing you say about me being an idiot is going to upset me because I'm at peace with myself." And you can replace idiot in this example with anything. It either has nothing to do with you, so it doesn't affect you, everything to do with you. You let it affect you, or it has to do with you, but it doesn't bother you or make you feel bad about yourself because you love yourself. You can choose which of these three responses you want to have. As you practice changing triggers into non-triggers, you will slowly become more and more emotionally intelligent. Eventually, you will not allow anything or anyone to bring your energy level down.

It's essential to recognize the things that trigger you. Find those triggers and keep them in your mind. Write them down if you must. Let yourself know that you don't have to be triggered by them, and think about why you don't need to be started by them. First of all, it will just send you into a primal state. In that initial state, you won't feel well; therefore, your happiness, production, creativity, and love for life will not be present with you. Your vibrational energy frequency will drop so that nothing good can happen because your energy is too low to see all the possibilities within your reality. Second, these negative thoughts do not hold truth in them. They're sending you into a fight/flight state. The only things that can be true and send us into this state are things that concern actual danger. So ask yourself how the opposite of those negative thoughts has more truth.

So, how do we get past reacting negatively? Well, by staying present. Being aware that we are the observer, the driver of the vehicle, and we can control our truck. That is the self-awareness step. Our bodies are the frame, and our mind is the computer (analytical mind) and the engine (subconscious mind). Our ego is the backseat driver complaining about everything. If we practice letting thoughts and feelings go, we can regain control over our mind and body from our autopilot. Right now, our mind and body are running the program of "they don't love me," "I'm not good enough," and "I can't change their mind". We must be greater than the program by taking back control and putting our hands on the wheel. That is the mindfulness step. So, if you look at a picture of your ex and you immediately feel the engine start to rev up, the windows start going up and down. The wheels start steering out of your lane, and you're used to letting the car do what it wants. So much so that half the time, you don't even recognize the car is reacting in a way you don't want it to, or if you do recognize it, you don't feel like you have any control over it. So, how do we gain control over it? Be the driver. Take the wheel. Steady the car back to a standard ride by calming the mind. Just let those thoughts scroll on. Ask the vehicle if it's done yet, and it will calm down. This mindfulness practice helps change our beliefs. And that's what we'll get into in the next chapter —changing beliefs one step at a time through self-awareness and mindfulness.

When we recognize that negativity lowers our energy and puts us in a primal state, we can start understanding that there is no truth behind the beliefs and the narrative going on in our heads to cause us to lower our energy. As we stop trusting our instincts and reactions, we begin being able to pause and think about it instead of going with what our programs are used to doing. This will cause us to feel free in a sense. We are no longer being a slave to our mind and body. But this new freeing feeling will also make us feel many negative things about ourselves, and we have to fight through that to reprogram ourselves. We will begin to see our faults, issues, bad habits, and negative thinking, which will be scary to observe.

It's like waking up and realizing you're in a horror movie and you're the villain. You'll want to hate yourself for your harmful programs and habits, but you don't have to hate yourself for it. You can focus on the fact that you will finally start cleaning up these bad habits and programs and turn your life around. It's always possible to start making positive changes within yourself and seeing positive changes in your life. We can't change our lives without first changing ourselves. It's not a quick process, but nothing rewarding is ever a quick process. Certain understandings may help us change our perspective and feel like we've leveled up our thinking. Still, a new perspective needs to change our habits and programs. Continuously using this unique perspective to help battle the old programs is where the magic happens slowly over time. The more effort we put into being mindful of these old programs, the faster we will begin to change. We can begin seeing our habits and beliefs as programs themselves. In that case, we become unphased by those programs. We can also begin putting our foot down regarding verbal abuse from our ego. "I'm no longer going to tolerate abuse from myself. I need to begin having a healthy relationship with myself, and it starts by no longer letting the ego be my bully." "I'm no longer going to allow myself to continue these bad habits of thinking, feeling, and doing. I'm going to make a change." Did anyone else hear Michael Jackson's song just now? We must keep looking at ourselves in the mirror and deciding to change what no longer serves us. It's not easy, but it's worth the challenge. Curiosity is a significant factor in helping our motivation. If we are curious about what our programs are in the first place, then we can be curious about what we can do to change them and what else we can accomplish by changing ourselves. "Wow, I don't let the weather bother me anymore. What else can I do?" "Wow, I'm not upset in traffic anymore. What else can I achieve?"

To end this chapter, we'd like to give you a few hacks that may help lift your mood throughout the day while you train your mind to do so. Once you've practiced enough, these tools won't be necessary. But in the meantime, it may help to use tools to keep your elevated emotions high. Keeping your feelings positive as often as possible is how you will become healthier without thinking about or manifesting it. Good thoughts and feelings yield good vibes and good energy within the body. This will signal the body to release the right hormones, proteins, chemicals, etc., that will help the body heal and function at its best. Patch Adams had the right ideas. "Laughter is the best medicine." Positivity is the best medicine.

Elevated Emotions Hacks:

-Listening to music you enjoy
-Listening to nature sounds
-Listening to frequencies or binaural beats
-Listening to meditation music
-Meditating
-Listening to an audiobook you enjoy
-Watching or listening to comedy
-Fake or real smiling
-Breath exercises
-Gratitude journaling
-Positive affirmations
-Daydreaming
-Acts of kindness
-Connecting with nature
-Creative expression
-Social connection
-Aromatherapy

Mindfulness Hacks:

-Stretching break relieves tension and grounds you in the present
-Savoring a hot beverage, sipping slowly with gratitude
-Gratitude Journal. Write down what you're grateful for. It shifts your focus to positivity
-Focus on mundane tasks instead of trying to get them over with as quickly as possible. Focus on your individual actions to stay present
-Conversation. Hearing each word as if you need to repeat it back to them and pausing before you speak. You can just collect your thoughts and respond instead of reacting.
-Stay aware of your surroundings and what you're doing, thinking, and feeling.

Hacks For Staying Present:
-Set alarms every 30 minutes as a presence check (make sure you're still aware and your energy is at a suitable frequency)
-Have soothing music or nature sounds or something going in your ear or the background
-The heart and smiling meditation we mentioned earlier

Things to reflect on:
-How long did you close up your heart? Keep it open and see how long you can do so.
-How long did you fall from grace today? How can you fall from grace for a shorter amount of time next time?
-What bothered you so much that your happiness wasn't as important anymore?
-Why did you let it bother you? What's the positive way to look at that situation instead so it doesn't bother you next time?

Our favorite mindfulness hack for keeping one foot in the 5D and one foot in the 3D is knowing that every moment is a synchronicity. It's all happening for a reason. And we manifested everything that's happening in our life right now. "Is this moment a lesson? What does it mean? Why is this exactly what I need in my life right now?" Thinking these kinds of thoughts about everything can really keep you aware of the 5D AND keep those elevated emotions going because YOU KNOW life is working FOR YOU, not AGAINST YOU. And it's fun to try to decipher why everything is happening when it does, even if we can't connect the dots fully at that moment. This kind of change in perception can help the "lows" in your life not get you down but instead create curiosity in each moment. This will help us keep an optimistic mindset even when things aren't going quite as smoothly for us. For instance, if you lose your phone, see it as a necessary moment. Maybe you'll find something else you lost while you're looking for your phone. Perhaps you needed to lose your phone for some other reason? But seeing losing your phone as nothing but an inconvenience, frustration, or a reason to be upset will lower your energy and cause you stress. Find the silver lining or try to build a fun, interesting, or curious narrative around the less fortunate things that happen to you.

CHAPTER 12: CHANGING BELIEFS

Now that you're becoming mindful of your thoughts, feelings, and habits, it's time to change your beliefs. Changing your beliefs is generally a process that takes time. We want to help you speed up this process by giving you tools to help. We went over mediation in an earlier chapter. This is your first step towards becoming aware of yourself. When you sit with yourself with no distractions, for no matter how long, you will start becoming aware of the patterns of your mind and body. Your body will start becoming anxious and antsy. It will want you to get up, move around, and do the same things you always do. Your mind will start telling you that this is a bad idea, that this is dumb, that you don't need to work on yourself, that you can't change, and that this whole meditation process isn't what you're used to, so stop doing it; it doesn't feel right, etc. So, the first step is becoming aware of these thoughts and feelings and seeing them objectively. Start seeing yourself from a 3rd person's perspective instead of a 1st person perspective. Be the player of the video game, not the video game character within the game. When that character tries to tell you what to do as the player, you don't have to listen because you're the one in control. So, the second step is to combat these negative thoughts and feelings with your analytical mind. You can fight it with logic. As we stated earlier, there are falsehoods in every negative thought. Understanding this allows us to dissect those thoughts and find the falsehoods logically. "That's too hard, I can't do it." Yes, you can do it; you can do anything. You either don't know how to do it, or you're just feeling fear of failure. You can figure out how to do anything, especially with the internet at your fingertips. You can also stop fearing failure because failure is a part of success. You can't have success without failure. Failure comes with the territory of success, so why worry about it? Embrace failure instead! If you fail, figure out what failed and why, and try something different next time. The next time, you will fail differently, and the time after that, you will have a new failure that you can learn from. Eventually, you will narrow down the process to the point where you no longer fail and finally succeed. If you let any failure stop you from progressing, learning, and growing, all your efforts are worthless. Your failures were a waste of time in the long run because you needed to keep going longer to achieve your desired success.

Once you can combat your negative feelings with logic, you no longer let them rule you. When a negative thought comes up, you dissect it and find the falsehood. Next time that thought comes up, you won't need to study it; you already know the falsehood, so you can stop listening to it. Then, a new negative thought presents itself. You dissect this new thought for its falsehoods. You're ready to dismiss it the next time that new thought presents itself. Your ego will degate you with more negative thoughts, which also will have falsehoods within them. Notice the falsehoods within each negative thing your ego wants to tell you. By having a debate in your mind against those negative beliefs and thoughts, you can uncover multiple false beliefs and thoughts within one single discussion. Your mind may say, "We can't do that; it's too hard!" And when you tell it that you can do it, it may respond with more false beliefs. "We're never going to change. We've been doing the same thing for years." Another negative falsehood is "We're never going to change." Yes, we are; everyone changes at some point. Change is a natural part of life; it is evolution. Change is going to happen even when we try to stop it. "But what if we fail? We'll be so embarrassed!" We are going to fail in some way. That's wonderful; we'll know what to do better next time! We can start thinking positively with logic alone; we don't have to bring the spirit/guide (angel on the shoulder) into the conversation to win this debate. That's the next step of changing beliefs, though. Bring in the positivity of the guide. The guide knows that we can forgive ourselves, forgive our negative thoughts, forgive our negative beliefs, forgive others who hurt us, and forgive life for the situations that have caused us trauma and grief. Once we stop letting our negative beliefs and thoughts win any debate, the next step is forgiving those old programs. Forgive ourselves for holding ourselves back.

Forgive those who hurt us because they either didn't mean to harm us or if they did, then it came from a hostile place within ourselves, and we can forgive them for that. We all make mistakes, and we can all grow from them. Even those who choose not to rise from their mistakes can be forgiven. If we don't forgive ourselves and others, we only harm ourselves. Drinking that poison of resentment expecting someone else to be broken by the poison we drink. We have to let it all go. Forgiveness is that last step, that previous level up in our growth of changing our beliefs—the last piece of the puzzle of becoming our best self. We'll explain these steps in detail in a later chapter so it's crystal clear.

This is how we can use short meditations to overcome our negative beliefs: Close your eyes and empty those thoughts. Put your awareness on nothing for a bit, and those thoughts in the mind and those feelings in the body will subside. Then, place your awareness on your breath and your heart. Breathe in and smile a bit. Your heart will start giving you elevated emotions of gratitude and love. Those emotions will fuel good feelings, and then those good feelings will fuel good thoughts. If you keep doing this, the car will start changing its autopilot to whatever you're making your new habits. If you're focusing on your heart more often and feeling great, your body and mind will follow suit. They will see that this is the new normal, so they will help you maintain that state. The mind will think positively, and the body will produce healthy hormones. Of course, at first, the car will keep doing what it's used to doing. But you're no longer on autopilot; you're at the wheel this time and can steer it. As you drive the vehicle, it will give in to your new driving habits. You're the kind of person who doesn't let things bother them now. You're the kind of person who works out regularly and eats healthily. You're the kind of person who thinks positively and does positive things for yourself and others. Those will become the norm as you keep correcting the old autopilot. And eventually, you can take your hands off the wheel, and your car will drive as you want. But why ever take your hands off the wheel? We'd rather stay in the driver's seat and enjoy the ride.

Live in the now as often as possible instead of living on replay. Instead of looking back at the end of the day on what you could have done better, you'll be looking at the now and deciding what you can do best for that moment. Recalling your mistakes is excellent so you can mentally rehearse what you will do better next time, but before you get to that step, you'll have to gain control over the negative thoughts. We can't let our mistakes drop us into lower energy and feed our negativity. "You don't lose by getting knocked down; you lose by staying down." -Muhammad Ali. At first, staying present will be challenging, and looking back at the replay will be very helpful as long as we don't let negativity take over. "Oh look, I messed up again. Gosh, I'm such a failure! Why can't I do anything right?" That's what's going to hold you back from growth. Instead, we think, "OK, I fell off the happy train at 6 pm because of what happened, and I never got back on the happy train. Well, what can I do differently next time? Next time, I can either find a way to get back on the happy train faster or stay present and keep myself from falling off in the first place. Why did I let that thing knock me off the happy train? That thing doesn't control me. I don't have to let it upset me. I won't let it next time." Next time, you'll be able to do this instead.

Find out what the emotion is by listening to the narrative that comes with the feeling. Sometimes, you'll know it's depression, anxiety, or fear. Other times, you may need to ask yourself what it is. This isn't too hard to determine; our emotions speak loudly and clearly. So when you do choose the emotion, start asking questions about it. "Where did this come from? Why am I feeling this way? Is this the past revisiting me? Is what I'm telling myself even true?" All beliefs are true. Both negative and positive. And you can choose to believe either one. To find out which ones you want to change from negative to positive and decide that there's no looking back. The windshield is much larger than the rearview mirror for a reason.

The graphic above shows the progression of changing beliefs and habits. Everything starts with intention and grows into being as we keep up with the process of rewiring our negativity into positivity. Mental rehearsal becomes practice. And practice becomes a habit. Habits become an attitude. An attitude becomes your personality. Your personality makes your reality. This all changes your beliefs/programs over time.

When you feel negativity infecting your mind and body, ask yourself, "Am I in danger right now? I feel like I'm in danger. Wait... Am I not in actual danger? Ok, well, something is wrong with my thinking then. Do I need to give in to this feeling? Does this feeling serve me? What is the narrative I'm hearing?" Whatever the narrative is, flip it and think about the opposite narrative. So if you're thinking you're a failure or that you suck, then think about how you're not a failure and how you don't suck. This is how we heal. As we work on the things we need to change, it will feel worse before it feels better. We'll notice so many things wrong with ourselves that we may feel it's too much to handle and change.

Think of this process as a fever. The fever has to happen to fight infection. It is heating the body so that it can kill the disease. And that heating up is rather uncomfortable for us, but the sickness must disappear. "The more you seek the uncomfortable, the more you will become comfortable." - Connor McGregor. The fever is the healing, but we don't like it, so we think negatively about it, just like anything else. When we go to the gym, we're excited to change. Then we feel sore and worn out and don't like that discomfort. So, we let that fear of that discomfort keep us from going back to the gym. But that fever, that feeling of pain, that soreness is precisely what has to happen to have success. The good thing is that all of those uncomfortable feelings will lighten up. Our body and mind will get used to this new habit over time and stop making us uncomfortable. With enough time and dedication, this new habit becomes the norm and no longer makes us uncomfortable. The same thing happens as we develop bad habits. It's awkward at first, and our mind and body try to stop us from changing our habit to this new lousy one. Still, we keep enforcing it, and it eventually becomes the norm. Reframing that belief is how we begin to shift the tides. If you can convince yourself you are healing and that this is just a fever the body has given you to heal itself, then the change process doesn't have to feel so scary. And changing for the better ends up inspiring us.

We begin wondering what else we can accomplish, which motivates us to keep changing and growing. Now, we're excited to find a new negative belief to get rid of and change over to a positive one. It becomes a snowball effect. We'll want to see more and more weeds to pick out of the garden of life that only hold that garden back from its potential. Change your beliefs, change your habits, change your programs, and you will change your life. It starts with us. We can't change anything else but ourselves. When we do change ourselves, we will change our reality in the process.

Another technique is to **Emphasize, Exaggerate, and Laugh**. So when you feel a negative emotion that creates negative thoughts within your mind, begin paying attention to those thoughts. Let yourself emphasize those thoughts and feelings by leaning into it all. Feel those feelings and let those thoughts grow. Start aware of where those thoughts lead you, their origin, and what's causing them. Now, exaggerate those thoughts and feelings so you can laugh about them. One of the simplest ways to accomplish this is by using a stand-up comedy routine. "I'm so ____!" "How ____ are you?" "I'm so ____, I ____!" Or "I'm so ____, I could ____!" Suppose you can laugh at yourself and laugh at a situation that's causing you stress. In that case, you can get past it and not feel owned by that situation and those thoughts and feelings that encompass it. Let's walk through some examples to illustrate the Emphasize, Exaggerate, and Laugh technique:

Situation: Feeling Overwhelmed at Work
- **Negative Thought:** "I have so much work to do; it's impossible!"
- **Emphasize:** Allow yourself to fully feel the weight of the workload.
- **Exaggerate:** "I'm drowning in a sea of papers! There's no way I'll survive!"
- **Laugh:** Create a humorous scenario like, "I'm so buried in paperwork; I need a snorkel at my desk!"

Situation: Relationship Woes
- **Negative Thought:** "We always argue about the same things."
- **Emphasize:** Dive into the frustration of recurring arguments.
- **Exaggerate:** "We're like professional arguers, going for the gold in the same topic!"
- **Laugh:** Lighten the mood with, "We argue so much, we should have our own reality TV show!"

Situation: Traffic Stress
- **Negative Thought:** "I hate being stuck in traffic; it ruins my mood."
- **Emphasize:** Feel the irritation of being stuck in the car.
- **Exaggerate:** "I'm trapped in my own personal parking lot; might as well set up camp!"
- **Laugh:** Imagine a comedic announcement, "Welcome to the 'Highway Standstill Comedy Hour!'"

Situation: Self-Criticism
- **Negative Thought:** "I always mess things up; I'm such a failure."
- **Emphasize:** Allow the weight of self-criticism to sink in.
- **Exaggerate:** "I'm the world champion of messing things up; it's my superpower!"
- **Laugh:** Turn it around with, "Watch out, world, here comes Captain Oops!"

Situation: Financial Stress
- **Negative Thought:** "I'll never get out of debt; it's hopeless."
- **Emphasize:** Feel the financial pressure.
- **Exaggerate:** "I'm in debt up to my eyeballs; might as well start a debt-themed fashion line!"
- **Laugh:** Picture yourself on a runway with clothes labeled "Credit Crunch Chic."

Remember, the goal is to shift the perspective and detach from the intensity of negative thoughts and emotions. Using humor and exaggeration, you create distance, allowing yourself to see the situation more lightheartedly. Our personality comprises how we think, feel, and act. So, to change our personality, we must change each of those three things at once. When you have a negative thought, think of the opposite positive thought. Then, act on that positive thought. Lastly, feel great about having that new positive thought and doing a new positive action. The action doesn't have to be anything significant; starting small is best. So, if you want to begin being a person, that works out. Think that you're capable of working out. Do a quick, short workout (even if it's something as easy as ten jumping jacks) and then feel great about it. Put your hand on your heart if necessary and feel that positive emotion. Connect that positive thought with a positive action and a positive emotion. This new habit now has a vote against your old habit. Your new habit has a leg in the race. And when you want to feel better about becoming that new person who works out now, you've got some proof to use against your old habit when your ego wants to tell you that you're never going to change. You can say, "Yes, I am. Look, I'm already doing it." Of course, your ego and subconscious aren't going to be convinced by one piece of proof or just one instance of you changing. Still, as you continue to reconfirm this new you, this new habit, and a new way of thinking, feeling, and acting, the ego and subconscious will have to give in and agree with you because the evidence has stacked up. You now have countless instances of proof that you have changed and that you can become a better version of yourself.

Now, do that with everything in your life. Replace old thinking, feeling, and acting with new thinking, feeling, and acting. Don't forget to add a feeling to that new thought and action. The feeling is what stamps that thought and action into your memory. If you just thought about working out and then did a quick workout and didn't feel good about it, then you're only going to reinforce the old habit, and you'll want to stop trying to work out. Why? Because you didn't associate this new habit with feeling positive. We'll talk more about feeling positive in the next chapter. Now that you're changing your mental and physical habits, another major part of the equation is that we must begin releasing negative energy instead of simply rewiring our thinking, feeling, and acting habits. At this stage, you are strong enough to control your life, but you will still have negative energy within you, which will keep surfacing repeatedly. You'll be able to handle it and shift into a positive mindset or mood, but we want to eliminate the negative energy within us so that this endless cycle doesn't continue. Let's get rid of that negative energy now. How do we do that? Through the heart!

CHAPTER 13: THE HEART

In this chapter, we want to express the importance of our hearts. We believe it to be our body's most important energy center. It is our source of elevated emotions, and we can tap into this emotional energy center at any time, like drawing energy from a battery. The heart is the zero point of our energy. It is the 4th energy center out of 7—three energy centers above it and three below it. The heart is also where we can find forgiveness, the emotion we'll need to tap into to release our negative energy continuously.

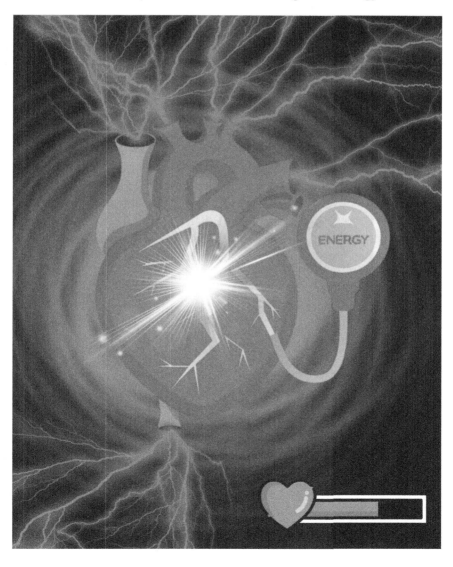

Understanding the profound connection between our heart and mind is pivotal. As we delve into the realm of heart coherence, we unveil the energies that shape our reality. Picture this: the symphony of your heart, conducting a melody intertwined with the pulsating rhythms of your thoughts. To fathom the depth of this connection, we embark on a journey through the impact of stress on our heart's coherence. When stress knocks on the door, triggering the release of potent chemicals, our heart responds rapidly. A primal instinct readies the body for a perceived emergency. Yet, in the modern world, it's often an email that serves as the catalyst, not a lion's pursuit. As the heart races in anticipation, we find ourselves simultaneously hitting the gas pedal and the brake. Our heart loses its harmonious beat in this paradox, and we plunge into incoherence. This departure of vital energy from the heart center into the adrenal realm disrupts our creative essence. We cease to create, imagine, and trust. Belief in ourselves and the vast realm of possibilities dwindles. In its incoherence, the heart becomes a silent spectator to the emotions of our future, stifling our innate urge to create.

Consider the conditioning by stress hormones – a silent force dampening our creative spirit. In moments of emergency, vulnerability becomes the enemy of survival. Past scars of heart-opening experiences echo caution, leading us to shield our hearts from potential bruises, manipulations, or exploitation. For those who've felt the sting of vulnerability, reopening the heart requires practice. Initially, the wellspring of emotions may seem distant, but with dedication, we can breathe life back into our hearts. As we cultivate emotions – be it fear, love, gratitude, or kindness – the heart emerges as the creative epicenter:

- A union of polarities, where opposites find unity.
- The genesis of wholeness.
- The gateway to our divine essence.

As energy flows back into the heart, orchestrating coherence, profound transformations unfold. The heart, a beacon of electromagnetic energy, extends its reach into the quantum field. An informational Wi-Fi signal emanates from the coherent heart, broadcasting our intentions – a vibrant electromagnetic signature pulsating with thoughts of wealth, health, and a new life. Sustaining heart coherence becomes an art – a daily practice of elevating emotions. As we master this practice, our bodies transcend the realm of stress, stepping into the harmonious balance. The subconscious mind, objective and malleable, believes in the emotions experienced, bridging the present with the future. A consistent practice of heart coherence opens the gateway to transformation. Independent of external influences, this practice births synchronicities, affirming alignment with our destined future. The energy synchronized with our aspirations beckons experiences, seamlessly materializing in our lives. Let gratitude, appreciation, thankfulness, and joy be the palette, and let heart coherence be the masterpiece painting our transformative journey.

Achieving Heart Coherence:

Step 1: Find a comfortable position and focus on your heart. Take slow, deep breaths, imagining each breath flowing in and out through your heart center. Hold your breath for a moment, then exhale gently through your heart. Feel the energy building in your chest. If your mind starts to wander, gently bring your attention to your heart and breath. As you continue this heart-centered breathing, your body will relax, and your brain will shift into coherent alpha brain wave patterns.

Step 2: Engage in heart-centered breathing and maintain it as you generate elevated emotions. Cultivate feelings of gratitude, appreciation, thankfulness, care, kindness, love for life, joy for existence, or freedom of expression. Practice experiencing these specific emotions as if your future goals have already been realized. By feeling these emotions in advance, you provide your body with a preview of the positive future you envision.

Step 3: Connect with a frequency or energy by radiating your intent from your heart. Feel a sense of connection with your heart, as if your future unfolds in the present moment. Instead of waiting for a specific event, recognize that you are already immersed in the emotions of your future. This connection to the energy of your future helps you experience a profound sense of being in the present while anticipating the positive outcomes ahead.

Distracting ourselves with thoughts of the new us might provide a momentary escape from old beliefs and emotions, but achieving genuine release demands a different strategy. It's common to believe that focusing solely on positive distractions will guide us away from negativity. However, we realize that more than merely hopping back onto the happy train is needed to eliminate the baggage of old beliefs and emotions. To authentically release the old collective self (the outdated programs, habits, thinking, and feeling), we must become comfortable with forgiveness. Embracing presence and mindfulness allows us to collectively listen to our shared body and mind without immediately reacting or avoiding it. Still, without forgiveness, these same problems from the ego will continue to plague us. We will have to continue to prevent or suppress them. So, if we've reached this journey where we can detect the falsehoods in the ego's narrative and then find the truths in the opposite positive narrative, the last step is to forgive that negative narrative as we choose to listen to the positive narrative. This gives the ego the recognition it needs without suppressing and upsetting it even more. Think of it as hugging your ego, calming it down, and telling it that it will all be okay and that you forgive it for overreacting. We have to treat ourselves like we're our best friends in the end instead of our mortal enemies. It may be productive at first to go to war with the ego to gain some confidence in fighting with it. Still, in the end, we must extend an olive branch between the soul and the ego so that our mind can work in harmony instead of continuing to be at war with itself.

This was an issue many of us had along our journey. We became too cold and stern with our egos, which yielded some results but not complete emotional freedom. The ego keeps coming back more and more upset about being suppressed. Many of us would end up being quite happy throughout most of the day, but as soon as someone or something knocked us off that comfortable train, we would become quite angry at that person, or that situation, or at ourselves for falling from grace or falling off the happy train. We'd think, "Well, I feel amazing; I'm in a great mood. It's that person's fault for knocking me off the happy train." This resentment would make our efforts futile and keep us wondering what else to do to grow and get beyond these reactions and this fear of falling off the happy train. "You can't stop the waves, but you can learn to surf," said Jon Kabat-Zinn. When we discover that forgiveness is the answer we've been looking for, we realize we don't have to worry about falling off the happy train.

We have become the comfortable train itself. The only person who can knock us off the tracks is ourselves, and we won't let ourselves do that anymore because we realize there's no point. "You are not a drop in the ocean. You are the entire ocean in a drop." -Rumi. There's no need to let things upset us, especially our ego. We can shake things off and keep feeling fabulous no matter what it is. We no longer have to wonder or worry if our day will end up good or bad. We're not gambling or chancing our emotional well-being. We're not rolling the dice and hoping for a good day anymore. We know we will have a great day because we consistently have the tools to make it happen daily. When we gain this ability, then we are no longer gambling. We are playing with house money, the casino's money. There's nothing to lose; there's no risk. Life is fun and full of beauty and surprises, and we're along for the ride. We're so excited to see how it all unfolds as we walk the path towards our dreams that we know will come true. That's a manifestation, and we'll cover that soon.

Imagine a collective feeling of depression suddenly engulfing us. Instead of accepting the narrative that "we suck," let's stay present, listen without emotional attachment, and collectively tune into our hearts. The best way to do this at any time of the day is to use the meditation exercise we gave at the end of the Meditation Chapter—deep, slow breaths. Focus on your heart; touch it physically if needed. A fake smile can help this process, too. Eyes closed if necessary. And listen to your heart. Talk to it if you'd like as well. Think about how much gratitude you have for your heart. The fact that it's keeping you alive by beating every second of the day. The fact is that it's our battery source for elevated emotions, and all we have to do is give it a little attention to feel much better. The more love we give our hearts, the more it gives us. And what a shame that we have ignored it so often in our lives. We find this relationship between heart and mind essential to build. With time, this simple exercise can be accomplished with little effort and very little time, seconds even. A couple of deep breaths and focusing on our heart can fill our elevated emotions meter right back up to the top in no time flat. Since thoughts and feelings work together, you can take the mental debate route with the ego or tune into your heart to induce positivity. Get yourself thinking positively, and you'll feel positive. Get yourself feeling positive, and you'll think positively. Eventually, you'll be able to accomplish these two goals simultaneously and start having complete control of your elevated emotions bar, keeping it full all day with ease. When it lowers just a bit, we can tune into our heart for a moment, and our emotions bar will return to the top.

The 4th center (our heart center) is the zero point. We mentioned the "zero point" at the beginning of this chapter. If you recall the picture we showed earlier in the book that showed the shape of the torus field, you can now see that the heart is at the center of that torus field within our own body. It's the middle center of our body and, therefore, where all our energy radiates. It's what fuels the other centers. There's no issue with focusing on it solely; it will be released to the other centers. And there's nothing wrong with giving attention to the whole body, though. But we see it as having one foot in the 5D and one foot in the 3D as often as possible. This expands our perspective and lets us keep the elevated emotions and deeper understandings present with us as we take in each new moment. The goal is to make each moment better than when it arrived. Enjoy every moment and make the most out of them.

We like to add this heart exercise to our mindfulness practice. Stay aware of our thoughts and feelings as usual, but add a little extra focus in the present moment towards our heart at all times, or at least as often as possible. Brush your teeth and pay attention to your heart. Take a shower and pay attention to your heart. Do the dishes and pay attention to your heart. Drive your vehicle and pay attention to your heart. Start incorporating awareness of your heart into every routine; this keeps you aware of your energy and your energy levels elevated. Again, once we feel some of our elevated emotions begin to fade, we can stop what we're doing and thinking and give our full attention to our hearts to fill that bar back up. But in the meantime, always keep an eye on the heart and remember how precious it is and how thankful we are for it being there for us not only as a life source but as a pick-me-up at all times of the day. It usually only takes a few seconds of entirely focusing on your heart for it to fill up your elevated emotions energy bank. Still, it also feels so good that we sometimes focus there for a while. It feels like "The Grinch" because our heart seems to be growing in 3 sizes, no joke. If you focus on your heart long enough, "your cup runneth over," and tears of joy may flow because you feel so much love for the world and life. Most of us authors cry every day now, and it's genuinely excellent. This little exercise may be less powerful for you in the beginning. There may be too many blockages in your energy flow to consistently feel better just from sensing the heart and feeling gratitude. Still, you can always get a little something out of this exercise, no matter how skilled you are with these practices we've discussed thus far.

Try starting with a few of these changes in perception:

-Life happens for us, not against us.

-We don't have to do anything; we GET to do things.

-It's not the moment in front of us that is bothering us; it's us that's bothering us about the moment in front of us.

-Everything happens for a reason; everything is a synchronicity. So why is this moment exactly what you need right now? What's the lesson? Why is it necessary for your journey? Even the less fortunate moments have meaning, and seeing things like that can create a constant optimistic perception.

-Life is silly; have fun with it. Chase excitement. When you make your next choice, choose the most exciting choice and do that until you can't anymore or until it loses its excitement, then repeat.

-Embrace your fears. It's a messenger trying to let you know that you have a negative/limiting belief within you that isn't aligned with your higher/best self. Find out what message fear is trying to deliver to you instead of ignoring or running away from it. It will keep ruling your life until you open the door and face it, so you might as well open the door now before it breaks down to confront you and deliver the message.

CHAPTER 14: SHADOW WORK

This may be the most crucial chapter in the book. Most people see the biggest and fastest results from shadow work. This step doesn't have to come late in the process. Still, we did want to explain many other things before we dive into this profound and uncomfortable technique. It will help to have self-awareness, mindfulness, and control over your emotions before taking on shadow work, but it's optional. Shadow work can be done at the beginning of this journey, too, and excellent results can come from it, but it takes work. The results are incredible and worth the rather painful and scary process.

Consciousness has often been compared to light. So, what is the opposite of light? Shadow. That means the shadow is essentially the unconscious. When we do shadow work, we're working with the subconscious mind, the aspects of ourselves that we don't know we don't know. Every child that is born is subject to socialization. The social group the child grows into has an idea of what is a good thing and what is a bad thing, what is acceptable and what is unacceptable. We're a social species, so what we want more than anything is that connection; we want to belong somewhere. But if we have a group of people exclaiming that if we want to belong and be close to that group, then XYZ is what we must see in you. We become very threatened by the aspects of ourselves that the social group does not accept. So what we do to be loved is hide all those aspects that we deem unacceptable as far as we can distance ourselves from them. So that we don't admit that it's even a part of us. We pretend that we don't possess XYZ to fit in and be accepted. This is part of the isolation that almost every person feels. We all know that we disowned an aspect of what is us to be a part of people's lives. So it's like we're all hiding the negative aspects of us. It's the Jekyll and Hyde complex.

Your shadow is essentially your dark side. It's the inner child within you that gets triggered by things. It's that part of the ego that is always upset, but this is more about your sore parts, yet you don't recognize them. Your shadow is the parts of you that you have disowned to survive and to progress through life without constant ache, pain, and trauma. It still gets triggered occasionally, and it wants your attention. We often dismiss this part of us because we don't want to think about it, and we don't want to own up to it. This is what continuously leads us to self-sabotage ourselves, though.

An example would be someone who has PTSD at a fireworks show. Everyone else is laughing, smiling, and enjoying the beauty of the experience. But the person with PTSD, who should have known better than to come to a fireworks show, is experiencing quite the opposite than those around them. Their shadow, deep within their subconscious, is triggered by the loud sounds and bright lights, and it's chasing them to relive the past instead of being able to enjoy the present moment. Another example of the shadow is that deep inner feeling that keeps us from succeeding because we're too scared to put ourselves out there and become judged for who we are.

Getting triggered is when someone or something brings up a part of us that we have disowned. And it causes us to have a reaction that's disproportionate to reality and the current situation. Most of us are Jekyll, who's been hiding the Hyde, and we don't want anyone to see it. So, it's the process of socialization that creates the subconscious mind. This drives us to feel like we are not enough as our authentic selves, so we depress parts of ourselves and become more and more inauthentic to fit in with society. Discovering the parts of us that we disowned can be tough. This exploration can feel like fumbling around with your hands in the dark, having no idea what you'll find inside yourself that you've been hiding this whole time. Venturing into the unknown can be scary, especially since these unknowns within us are the things we didn't like about ourselves in the first place. But our reality is full of us, so we will only find more of ourselves in the unknown. So why fear knowing more about us?

Always remember that you're the soul/observer inside this avatar that the ego runs. And treat the ego like an abused/neglected child because that's precisely what we've done to it most of our lives. We have disowned parts of us and shoved them away. The ego isn't solely negative or positive. However, it does speak for the subconscious. When there's still deep-seated pain within our subconscious, it will constantly self-sabotage us. The child inside us wants love and attention and to cry it out, but we keep ignoring it or telling it to shut up, quit whining, and put a smile on. Children need love and attention and for someone to tell them it will all be okay, they don't have to be in pain anymore because that's in the past, not the present. When we no longer fear our triggers, we can finally own them, acknowledge them, comfort them, forgive them, and then release that pain.

We can try to poke the "bear" or trigger our inner child on purpose with shadow work and by doing things we fear, but remember not to push through it; instead, offer comfort, understanding, and forgiveness to that inner child when they want to freak out. We can also stay aware at all times, and when we feel triggered, handle it with care. We don't necessarily have to poke the bear. Still, it will release those fears, traumas, and negative/limiting beliefs much faster than waiting the next time we get triggered. BECOME AWARE OF THE BEAR! Then comfort it and let it become a teddy bear instead of a terrifying bear.

As our guide (spirit) begins guiding and teaching the ego, the ego releases its fears and traumas and slowly becomes our cheerleader. Let the guide be the parent to the damaged ego. This way, it can grow into a healthy adult and stop sabotaging its avatar as it tries to level up. Also, realize that as the observer/soul, we are whole of love no matter what happens. Other people's approval shouldn't increase our self-esteem, nor should their disapproval decrease our self-esteem. We don't need others' validation to feel whole. Giving others the keys to happiness means we are no longer responsible for our lives and feelings. Same for success and wealth and fame and all that materialistic crap that the soul cares nothing about. We're just here to experience and grow. To love and learn. Forgiveness is the key to living a loving life with no boundaries or limitations holding us back. Life is about creation, and we are the creators of whatever we want to do with this life. Shed the past so the future becomes full of unlimited possibilities by releasing and eliminating our limiting beliefs.

Become aware of when you're being triggered. Being triggered is when your response is disproportionate to reality. You can't just try to create an environment that doesn't start you, and you can't fight when you get triggered (desensitize). Both of these will lead back to the same issue. Stop fighting or avoiding it; own it, accept it, acknowledge it, and dive into why it's there. Then forgive and let go. When we're triggered, something we have disowned is being poked at inside us. Instead of continuing to disown it, we must own it and begin understanding it to change it. Instead of reframing our beliefs, we need to identify everything that has convinced us that the assumption is valid. Let go of all the things that are maintaining that belief. You can think of a negative belief like a table. Instead of banging on the table with a bat and trying to break it down forcefully or ignoring the table completely, we want to figure out what's keeping it stable. Look at the legs and begin dismantling them so the table no longer has legs to stand on.

Shadow work is not about trying to get rid of the blockages; it's about investigating the belief systems that you bought into and identifying those beliefs so that you can recognize that the beliefs that are out of alignment with your truth don't belong to you and you can let them go. Parents, friends, or society may have given you them, but once you identify them as someone else's beliefs, you will understand that they don't belong to you, and you can let them go. You let them go because you don't want to carry what doesn't belong to you. So let them go if they don't belong to you. Because once you understand that they don't belong to you, they have no more effect on you. The impact is only what you choose to be affected by. And if you have unconscious beliefs, you feel the impact because you're unaware of the belief. When you know what the belief is, once you identify it, it no longer has an effect.

Growth is the process of inclusion, not exclusion. You will always be aware of things as possible experiences. Still, you can understand that you don't have to buy into any experience of the past to buy into the you that you're experiencing now. If you define yourself as a new person, then wouldn't you, as a new person, have a different past than the person who was there a moment ago? The past does not define the present unless you choose to create that illusion. The present should represent the past and redefine that past. Repaint that dark childhood into a beautiful past that needed to happen for you to learn to be the whole self you are today. To understand the lessons you did and become closer to being the genuine, authentic you. "The pain wasn't your fault, but the healing is your responsibility."

As we venture into the unknown, we don't have to fear it. Our entire reality is made up of us. How we perceive everything, think, feel, act, react, etc. So, by venturing into the unknown, we will genuinely only find more of ourselves. As we shine our flashlight of awareness into the darkness of the unknown, the only thing awaiting us is more of us. We will only discover more things about ourselves. That may seem scary, but it doesn't have to be. It can be viewed as exciting. The more you know about yourself, the more you can navigate life in the best way possible. We can't change things about ourselves until we become aware of them. The only way to become aware of them is to venture into the unknown. So, look for your shadow with excitement instead of fear. Remove your negative energy with excitement instead of fear. It's all part of the growth process. Make mistakes and be excited about making mistakes because you can learn from them and do better the next time. Embrace being wrong, embrace failing, embrace being upset. We can learn from and grow from every one of these things.

Once we learn to forgive, we can release those negative/limiting beliefs from our subconscious. We discussed this in the ego section and want you to visualize your heart as a jar of light now. That light is clouded by the smoke of negativity within us. The only way to open that jar is with forgiveness. We can't ignore the jar and expect the light to shine through; we can't bang on the jar, and we can't scoop out the smoke of negativity. The only way to release it is by opening the lid and investigating the smoke within. When we forgive ourselves and others for the negativity we have within, that smoke begins to release from the jar. Eventually, all that's left is light, and it shines brighter than ever because all the smoke has cleared.

We want to get into our three types of minds briefly. The concepts of the socialized mind, self-authoring mind, and self-transforming mind are derived from the work of psychologist Robert Kegan. These ideas are part of his adult development theory, particularly outlined in his book "The Evolving Self." Kegan's theory suggests that individuals progress through different cognitive and emotional development stages.

Socialized Mind:

Description: At the socialized mind stage, individuals are primarily shaped by external influences, societal norms, and the expectations of others. They conform to the values and beliefs of their immediate social environment. The sense of self is strongly tied to external approval and conformity to societal norms. There needs to be more capacity for independent, critical thinking.

Characteristics: Conformity, dependence on external approval, adherence to societal norms, limited capacity for independent thought.

Self-Authoring Mind:

Description: In the self-authoring mind stage, individuals develop a sense of internal authority and differentiate their values and beliefs from external influences. They become more capable of defining their principles and goals. This stage involves a greater capacity for introspection, self-reflection, and taking ownership of one's life.

Characteristics: Developing internal values, ability to define personal principles, increased self-awareness, taking ownership of one's life.

Self-Transforming Mind:

Description: The self-transforming mind represents a more complex level of development where individuals can hold and integrate conflicting ideas and values. They can see multiple perspectives and adapt their views based on new information. This stage involves a high degree of cognitive flexibility, tolerance of ambiguity, and the ability to manage complexity.

Characteristics: Cognitive flexibility, ability to integrate conflicting perspectives, tolerance of ambiguity, capacity to manage complexity.

Individuals may need to fit into a single stage neatly, and the progression through these stages is sometimes linear. People may simultaneously exhibit characteristics of multiple phases, and personal development is lifelong. Kegan's framework provides a valuable lens for understanding the evolving nature of human consciousness and how individuals make meaning of their experiences at different points in their lives.

Most people find themselves in the social mind state. This is your mind during your teenage high school years when you're looking at others and thinking, "Where do I fit in? Who are the cool kids? Am I popular? How can I impress the popular kids?" I always wanted to fit in but have yet to stand out. You want to be a part of the group. The level above that is self-authoring, when you look within instead of at others. This also isn't the ideal mindset because you look within and not at others. The self-transforming mind is the mindset you have when you can see the limitations of both of the other perspectives. You listen and trust yourself but are still open to external feedback and not blind to it.

Again, most people are in the socialized mind. "Society tells me what to think, what to do, how to fit in, what my goals are." Even in your decisions, it's not, "What do I care about?" It's instead, "What will impress people?" Same with partners in relationships. Not, "What do I want?" It's instead, "What will society think is cool? Can I brag about my partner to society?" In this mindset, you're not living or thinking for yourself. So, in the end, it's part of growing up. Yes, maybe younger you were stuck there, but current you, while honoring and loving younger you, it's time to grow beyond that. "Well, what do I value? What do I care about? What's real to me?" Also, this idea of living up to your potential can keep you from growing. There's always another potential. Aim for your potential, but don't set it as a requirement to love yourself. Your potential is you, right here, right now. Who decides if your body is perfect or not? You do; it's your reality.

Listen to yourself and stay true to yourself. Consider every decision: "Does this feel authentic to me?" The most prominent feeling you'll sense when it is authentic to you is that you feel more at home within yourself. Unauthentic thoughts and actions always feel like you're betraying yourself and moving further away from you. The feelings your body gives you in response to your actions will reveal whether you're acting authentically or unauthentically if you listen to your body. True confidence is relaxing and feeling at home, not like you must improve on something to feel better about yourself. In the end, tell yourself it's okay to be you. It's okay to be you and not let anyone convince you otherwise. Your mind convinces you that only you are going through specific struggles and that no one else can relate. But we are all going through so many struggles.

Here is a list of shadow questions you can try on yourself:

Why did my parents hurt me, and why is it entirely my fault?
Why am I not good enough?
Why do I need to be better?
What's missing in me?
What do I hate most about myself?
What do I hate about my body?
What would I change if a genie could magically change one thing about me?
Why is no one going to love me?
Why am I a disappointment to myself?
Why is success not for me?
Why is my fear scary?
Why don't I deserve happiness?
Why is success not for me?
What am I hiding?
Why does life have to be hard for me?
When did I stop loving myself?
What's so hard about loving myself?
Why have I yet to start loving myself?
Why am I unlovable?
What have I always hoped someone would tell me in life?

Whatever gets triggered there, let go of it. But remember that even with letting go, you can fall into the trap of "I need to let go of everything to fix myself," but letting go isn't about fixing yourself. Letting go is about realizing that there's nothing to fix. It's letting go of all the lies you bought into about yourself. So it's not "I need to fix all of this." What if you're not broken, and it's all an illusion? Underneath it all, you were good enough and while to begin with. Fix the ego within your avatar so you can succeed more in life without self-sabotage holding you back anymore, but don't see that goal as something that has to happen for you to be whole, worthy, good enough, excellent, etc. You're already all those things; you may need some shadow work to realize it.

Here are some questions to ask yourself to help yourself to help dismantle these limiting beliefs:

How do these beliefs influence my thoughts, behaviors, and choices?
What evidence do I have that contradicts these limiting beliefs?
What would my life look like if I no longer held onto these beliefs?
What stories or narratives am I telling myself that contribute to these limiting beliefs?
Can I identify a specific event or experience that may have contributed to the formation of these beliefs?
What advice would I give to someone else in my exact same situation?
What would I do if I knew I couldn't fail?
What/who do I need to start saying no to?
Who do I need to forgive?
Who am I still angry at?
What have I changed my mind on?
What seemed essential to me years ago that doesn't now?
Why do I feel that I can't fully love and accept myself for me in my inner core, not just my accomplishments and what I've done?

What if there's nothing wrong with me?
What if I'm not broken?
What if there's nothing to fix?
If I stopped self-sabotaging myself with _____, I'd
accomplish _____. I accept no more excuses from myself.

If someone disapproves of you right now, what does that trigger? Probably rejection. So why is that bad? You probably wouldn't feel good because of it, but that's not how it has to work. If we logically analyze this, what does it imply? That you're a slave to other people's approval. So you're saying other people hold the keys to your self-worth. That's not good. So how do you become good enough? How do you reclaim that? Who says you're good enough in the end? Not anyone else; it's you, yourself. So, are you good enough if others disapprove of you? YES. Are you enhanced if others approve of you? No, you're not. Other people's opinions of you should not affect your self-esteem and worth. Taking criticism with a grain of salt to help yourself better analyze things in your life or things about yourself that you may not have recognized can be great, but solely relying on other's opinions is a losing battle for your self-worth. If everyone boos you, you're okay. If everyone cheers for you, you're also okay; that's freedom. Being yourself without needing anything from the outside world is true freedom.

It may help to say to yourself, "I'm not run by disapproval nor approval of others!" Instead of faking it until you make it, try acting authentic until you remember who you are. Julien Blanc has beautiful videos and seminars that explain and expand upon this kind of information. We highly recommend that you check him out! Realize that everything in your life right now you secretly love, or you would have gotten rid of it already or done something about it. However, you're not always aware of the part of you that loves it. So, when it comes to self-sabotage, instead of trying to fight against it, it's much more beneficial to identify the part of you that loves it. So, for example, if you're terrified of what people think of you, deep down, but consciously, you think, "If people love me, then I wouldn't have to worry so much. So I want people to love me!" But for people to love you, you must put yourself out there and be vulnerable to their opinions. And if you put yourself out there, you can and will be judged. So you're going to hold back even though consciously you want to be more sociable; you won't do it to avoid the more profound fear. It's the same with being successful. If a part of you believes you're irresponsible, "Look, I can't even clean my room; I'm not responsible at all," then you won't allow yourself to become successful and responsible. Your subconscious limiting beliefs will work against you and sabotage your success because you don't believe you're responsible enough to be successful.

Self Sabotage will always be congruent with your comfort zone or underlying beliefs. So we would ask you, "Yes, a part of you wants to live up to that potential, but another part doesn't. Why? Why is living up to your potential bad or scary? Why do you secretly not want to? Why do you secretly love staying in your comfort zone? Then you may say, "Fear of rejection." This means you'd figuratively rather cut off your hand than your arm. That's how it works. You'll never do something you don't think is the best option. But now you have found what's holding you back in the case of living up to your potential: Fear of rejection. Now you're aware of it and can begin working on releasing that fear of rejection by confronting it, analyzing it, and realizing that you no longer need to fear rejection. That will create a paradigm shift within you so you can begin living up to your potential.

Well, what about bad habits like smoking? We'll reiterate what we said earlier. You're smoking, and you'll choose to cut off the hand each time (smoking the cigarette). You're smoking to avoid something else that feels much worse. You know it's terrible, but it feels much worse not to smoke and then deal with all the stress of whatever you're trying to numb with smoking. So, what is the actual, more profound fear? Stress. But the nicotine addiction is actually what's causing you to feel stressed in the first place when you don't have enough nicotine in your system. So when you realize that, you can see that quitting smoking will be less stressful for you in the long run. It may be stressful for a little while, but in the long run, you will no longer be in that negative stress loop that smoking constantly causes.

Let's try an example of having a fear of rejection. So, what's so scary about rejection? When did you start holding yourself back from being rejected? What happened? You may devise an example of when you didn't feel like you belonged somewhere. So, what made you think that way? You will likely have a clear example in your mind of something said or done to you that made you feel rejected. How did this idea that you don't belong then follow you in life, and where has it resurfaced? Perhaps you got diagnosed with anxiety, and that became your excuse for not having to heal that or look deeper at the issue. Now, when you get triggered by something that makes you feel fear of rejection, you can chop it up to your diagnosis and not do anything about it. Instead, you can now find comfort in accepting who you are. That's unhealthy, though, and will continue to be your scapegoat in life. Anxiety can be worked out of your system in time; it doesn't have to own you. So what would your mind or body say if someone were to tell you that there's nothing wrong with you and nothing broken within you? You may want to believe it, but most likely, some don't fully believe it. You want to see what parts of you don't think it. What response comes to your mind when that question is asked of you? What's the objection within you? Look past the easy answer and find the one that hurts to say. Also, look past the "I don't know" answer because you do know; you have to dig deep and find that voice inside you (the ego speaking for the subconscious) and what it says in response to these shadow questions. It may feel like you're going around in circles, but challenge yourself to go deeper, peel that layer back and find the pain inside.

In the journey of self-discovery and personal development, many individuals find themselves caught in a cycle of self-sabotage, often perpetuated by the invisible boundaries of a self-imposed ceiling and floor. This chapter delves into the psychological intricacies of self-sabotage, exploring the dynamics of comfort zones, the role of limiting beliefs, and the transformative power of recognizing one's inherent worthiness. We want to break this down more and explain what's causing it and how to break free from self-sabotage.

The Comfort Zone:
- A comfort zone is a psychological space where individuals feel at ease, unchallenged, and safe. Within this zone lies a perceived ceiling, limiting what one can achieve or experience comfortably. Going beyond this ceiling often triggers the subconscious mechanisms of self-sabotage, designed to bring them back to the familiar and comfortable space they've grown accustomed to.

The Ceiling and the Floor:
Ceiling: The ceiling represents the upper limit of what individuals believe they deserve or can achieve. It is a self-imposed boundary that, when breached, triggers self-sabotaging behaviors to restore a sense of control and familiarity.
Floor: Conversely, the floor signifies the lowest point an individual is willing to tolerate. A wake-up call occurs when they fall below this point, prompting a desire for change and self-improvement.

The Cycle of Self-Sabotage:
- The self-sabotage cycle begins when individuals approach or surpass their perceived ceiling. Fear, doubt, and the discomfort of the unknown arise, compelling them to revert to familiar patterns, even if those patterns hinder progress. Conversely, dropping below the floor activates a survival instinct, prompting a recognition of the need for change and motivation to rise above.

Shifting the Perspective:
- Rather than perpetuating the cycle of thinking that improvement is necessary to feel worthy, a transformative shift in perspective is essential. Recognizing that inherent greatness and worthiness are constants, irrespective of achievements or setbacks, is a pivotal realization. The key lies in identifying and dismantling the limiting beliefs and societal conditioning that create the illusion of unworthiness.

Cutting the Ties:
- Understanding the root causes of limiting beliefs is crucial to breaking free from the self-imposed box. These beliefs often stem from societal expectations, past traumas, or inherited thought patterns. By identifying these influences and consciously cutting the ties that bind, individuals can liberate themselves from the constraints that have held them back.

Success Beyond Limits:
- Once the ties are severed, individuals can transcend the limitations of their perceived ceiling. Success then becomes a natural outgrowth of self-expression rather than a constant pursuit driven by a need for external validation. Embracing the truth of inherent worthiness empowers individuals to live authentically, tapping into their full potential without the constraints of self-sabotage.

Conclusion:
- Breaking free from the cycle of self-sabotage requires a profound shift in mindset and a commitment to self-awareness. By acknowledging inherent greatness, understanding the dynamics of comfort zones, and courageously cutting the ties to limiting beliefs, individuals can unleash their full potential and achieve success beyond the confines of ceilings and floors they once thought defined them. The journey is not about becoming worthy; it's about recognizing and embodying the worthiness that has always existed within.

Many assume we're not good enough, and it gets programmed into us. Then, it hijacks our RAS (Reticular Activating System) or your selective focus. So now you filter the world through the lens of, "I'm a little different. I'm someone for whom things may not work out." And what's that going to do to your life? You're going to start looking for proof consciously. It is the same as someone who is always scared and looking for threats. And when you find evidence, it reinforces that limiting belief. That negative belief then continues to hijack your focus even more. Then you may seek self-help, and you can easily get sucked into this whole "I need to improve. I need to get better" mindset. And that reconfirms your limiting belief. But really, there's nothing to be fixed.

So, as long as you keep trying to improve yourself from the assumption of "I am broken," it will follow you forever. Shadow work isn't "I'm broken. How do I fix myself?" It's realizing that you were never broken in the first place; it was all lies and conditioning. You don't need to improve yourself; you're already enhanced. You don't need to become enough; you are enough. It would help to let go of the lies that made you feel you were broken so you can realize you weren't actually broken from the start. You just began carrying baggage that wasn't yours. Try to get naked in front of the mirror and say, "I love you," and notice if any part of you isn't okay with it. Don't lie to yourself. Can you say "I love you" and "I love my body" without a part of you feeling like it's lying? You can start processing those sensations and let go of them. Then try every part of your body and say you love that. Let go of it. "Letting go" meditations work well too. What we seek out in the world, more often than not, is what we seek inside ourselves. So, if you're trying to seek approval, you're seeking approval because you think that if people out there love you, then you can love yourself. But that's the backward way of accomplishing self-love, which will never work. It's an endless cycle of pain. Because even if most of the world loves you, the few that don't will reinforce that limiting belief that you don't deserve love, and you'll self-sabotage again.

People do this with their partner, too, and think, "If this person only loves me more, then I can love myself." It's the same: "I'm gonna try to control people and control how they think and react to me and control life so that I can just feel safe." These two examples go back to the law of polarity. The first example is how empaths feel and act. The second example is how narcissists feel and act. The narcissist thinks to themself, "I need to create this safe space around me to create a predictable outcome or reality." But what you're seeking is safety within. If you felt whole within, it wouldn't matter what happens outside yourself; you could handle it. Sometimes, you think, "I'm not good enough," and you withdraw from loving yourself because you're in a relationship with yourself; everyone is. Now, most people are in very abusive relationships with themselves. We all have an inner child. Most of us are just abusing that inner child.

Shadow work is a way for us to begin no longer abusing our inner child. Instead of abusing or neglecting that inner child, we must show it love, care, and comfort and teach it the right way of thinking and feeling to grow up and become a healthy adult. In the end, this is you. This reality, this is you. You have a choice: you can resist life or embrace it. You can resist you or welcome you. You will still look the same whether you fight you or hug you. So what's going to lead to a more joyful life? Embracing it. You can have intentions and goals out of inspiration, but in the end, what's so bad about the right here right now? Nothing; Nothing at all. Put your foot down on any inner self-abuse. When you think something like, "Okay, I'll do that exercise," and in response, your inner child/ego tells you, "Who are you kidding? Look at yourself," don't accept that narrative from yourself. You are your greatest abuser. What if someone in the real world treated you the way your inner voice treats you? Would you still hang out with them? Think of that inner voice as the worst person ever alive at first if you have to. You could be having a great day, and then suddenly, that inner voice says, "Remember that thing that happened when you were nine years old, and it was so embarrassing?" That ends up poisoning the moment. What if you had a friend like that? No matter how well things were going, they brought back the negative. You'd get rid of that friend, right? We sure hope you would.

People think, "Isn't that resisting yourself?" No, it's setting a boundary for yourself (self-love and self-respect. Why let yourself be abused?) You can't stay in this space of hating your inner child; it's a stepping stone to create enough space to process and let go of it. Once you regain control over the internal abuse that's happening and have distanced yourself from believing everything it says to a point where it constantly lowers your energy, then you can begin listening to it and having a conversation with it. Investigate what's keeping that negative belief alive and see that it was all from past experiences that no longer affect you. Then, you can forgive the people who hurt you, place those negative beliefs within your subconscious, and forgive yourself for carrying that weight around this whole time. Then, that negative energy and negative belief will finally be released. It'll take several instances of continuing to coach your ego. Still, with each release, the pain becomes more accessible to deal with the next time. It won't be nearly as hard to talk with yourself about that darkness within you and then rerelease it. Soon enough, the darkness will be gone completely.

LEVELS OF CONSCIOUS TRANSFORMATION

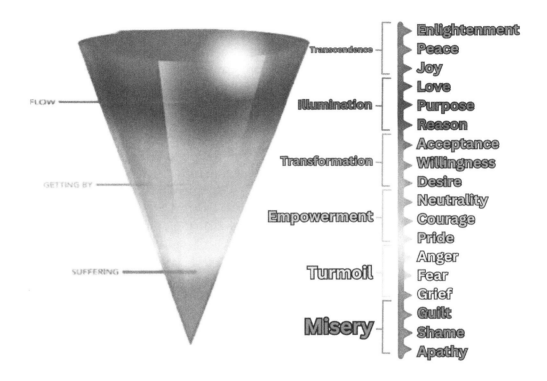

Many people have seen similar charts to the one above. It's typically called the "Levels Of Consciousness" chart. We've transformed it and rearranged a few levels into what you see here. These levels are grouped into threes; you can move up 1-3 levels simultaneously. You, for sure, can't move up more than that. So, you either move up one level or category as you heal yourself emotionally. As you move up, you're going to need different advice. Try to feel a level just above where you're at or a level within a category above where you're at now. So, suppose you're feeling apathy (hopelessness). In that case, you want to feel some other form of misery like guilt, shame, or maybe even something in the Turmoil category. If you try to induce an emotion any higher than that, you will fall back down the scale.

So generally, if you're feeling apathy, you either want to allow yourself to feel shame or guilt for what you've done that made you give up. This can then lead you to feel grief for the things you've done and possibly fear of repeating your mistakes. Then, you can feel anger towards yourself or someone else to keep moving up the scale. Somewhere in these bottom two levels, you can start feeling like a victim, which is better than a monster or quitter but still not ideal. Next, you can find a sense of pride and courage to step up. This can lead to desire and willingness to do better for yourself and others. Then, you can accept your faults and mistakes and begin reasoning with yourself. This can help you find purpose in life. Once you've found purpose, you can start chasing your dreams and feel love, joy, and peace. When you've handled those enough, you can eventually become fully enlightened. So there's different advice to give yourself and others depending on where you or they are on this scale. If you try to tell someone who feels shame to love themselves, it will be horrible advice and won't do anything for them. Understand where you're at on the scale so you can help yourself or others move up this scale of transformation. Also, realize that you may feel rather high on this scale when it comes to one aspect of life but relatively low when it comes to another. For instance, you could be successful and feel great about that. Yet, you need to improve in the relationships department. The opposite could be true as well. So, know where you're at with each aspect of life to move up the scale effectively.

We each have an overall placement on this scale when considering all aspects of our lives. Still, within individual elements, we may be all over the scale. Do your best to understand where you are on this scale for all aspects, and then use this scale to help yourself transform and move up the scale. The ego is what keeps us on the bottom half of this scale. Once we recognize the deception and wrong way of thinking within the ego and release it, we can climb to the top half of this scale. The outside world will only satisfy us once we are ready to take this inner journey. When we grow beyond the ego and realize we are the soul/observer, we transcend the ego and climb into the upper scale of the levels of conscious transformation.

Before we move on to the next chapter, we'd like to introduce you to the "Immunity Map" created by Robert Kegan and Lisa Laskow Lahey in their book, "Immunity to Change." They present the
concept of the immunity map as a tool to understand and overcome personal resistance to change. The immunity map is a structured process that helps individuals identify and challenge the internal barriers that prevent them from making desired changes in their behavior or mindset. Here is a detailed explanation of the immunity map:

Immunity Map:

1. Identify the Improvement Goal:
- Start by clearly defining the change or improvement goal you want to achieve. Be specific about the behavior, mindset, or outcome you aim to change.

2. Identify Current Behaviors:
- List the current behaviors or actions counterproductive to the desired change. This involves being honest about what you currently do that goes against your stated goal.

3. Identify Competing Commitments:
- Explore the competing commitments that are driving the undesired behaviors. These are the hidden, often subconscious, commitments that conflict with your stated goal. Competing commitments are fears, anxieties, or beliefs that operate beneath the surface.

4. Uncover Hidden Competing Commitments:
- Use inquiry and reflection to uncover the deeper commitments holding you back. Ask yourself questions like:
- What am I afraid might happen if I change?
- What beliefs or assumptions am I holding onto that conflict with my goal?

5. Identify Big Assumptions:
- Big assumptions are the deeply ingrained beliefs that fuel your competing commitments. These are often long-standing beliefs that have become automatic and may not even be conscious. Identify the assumptions that underlie your competing commitments.

6. Test the Assumptions:
- Challenge and test the validity of these significant assumptions. Are they accurate? Are they still applicable in your current context? This step involves a process of critical examination and self-inquiry.

7. Create Experiments:
- Design and implement small experiments to test whether your significant assumptions hold true. These experiments are concrete actions or practices that challenge old beliefs and allow you to gather real-world evidence.

8. Reflect and Iterate:
- Reflect on the outcomes of your experiments. Did your assumptions prove accurate, or did the evidence suggest otherwise? Iterate the process by adjusting your assumptions, creating new experiments, and continuing the cycle if necessary.

The immunity map is powerful because it helps individuals uncover and address the hidden forces that resist change. By systematically examining competing commitments and significant assumptions and testing those assumptions through small experiments, individuals can gain insights into their own resistance and develop strategies for overcoming it. The process is designed to be repetitive, encouraging continuous learning and adjustment based on real-world feedback.

The last thing we want to cover related to shadow work is QHHT, Quantum Healing Hypnosis Technique. It's similar to shadow work but dives even more profoundly than shadow work. Shadow work can be done independently, but having a therapist to guide you down into your Subconscious is better. You do not have to be in a hypnosis state to achieve results through shadow work, though. Dolores Cannon, a renowned hypnotherapist and author, developed a technique known as Quantum Healing Hypnosis Technique (QHHT). This approach focuses on accessing the client's past lives and higher consciousness to facilitate healing on physical, emotional, and spiritual levels. Here's an in-depth explanation of Dolores Cannon's QHHT:

Quantum Healing Hypnosis Technique (QHHT):

Past Life Regression:
- QHHT often begins with a past life regression. The client is guided into a deep state of relaxation and heightened awareness. In this altered state, they can access memories from past lives that may relate to their current life situations and challenges.
Subconscious Exploration:
- As the session progresses, the focus shifts to the client's Subconscious, often referred to as the Subconscious Higher Self or the "SC." This part of the mind is believed to hold vast information about the individual's life purpose, lessons, and the root causes of current issues.
Communication with the Subconscious:
- Through a series of questions, the practitioner communicates directly with the client's Subconscious. The Subconscious is considered a wise and all-knowing aspect that can provide insights, guidance, and healing.
Identification of Physical Issues:
- The practitioner directs the Subconscious to identify and explain physical ailments or health issues the client is experiencing. This process aims to uncover the root cause of the problem, which may have origins in past lives, current life traumas, or emotional blockages.

Healing Interventions:
- Once the causes are identified, the Subconscious is asked to facilitate healing. This can involve various interventions, such as energy healing, balancing, and releasing emotional traumas. The Subconscious tailors the healing process to the individual's specific needs.

Life Guidance and Insights:
- Beyond physical healing, QHHT seeks to provide broader life guidance. Clients may learn about their life purpose, relationships, and personal growth. The Subconscious often imparts wisdom and perspectives that can be transformative.

Integration and Awakening:
  - Toward the end of the session, the practitioner helps the client integrate the experiences and insights gained. Clients often report a sense of empowerment, clarity, and a shift in their perception of challenges.

Key Principles:

Holistic Healing:
- QHHT views the individual as a holistic being, addressing physical, emotional, and spiritual aspects to promote comprehensive healing.

Higher Consciousness:
- The technique emphasizes connecting with the client's Higher Self or Subconscious, regarded as the individual's higher, wiser aspect.

Individualized Healing:
- Healing is tailored to each individual's unique needs and experiences, recognizing that everyone's journey is distinct.

Dolores Cannon's QHHT has gained popularity for its transformative potential, offering a unique and profound approach to healing by tapping into the depths of the subconscious mind and higher consciousness. There are many QHHT practitioners nowadays; the same goes for shadow work practitioners. Julien Blanc is our collective favorite in the shadow work realm. You can find both of these teachers on YouTube. These two types of work that help us dig into our Subconscious profoundly help with our transformative journey. We highly recommend researching and trying both techniques. Now that we've gone through all the steps to conquer the ego and begin releasing your limiting beliefs and negative energy trapped inside your Subconscious, we will move on to other transformative methods that will help you in life. If you only learned things up to this point, you'd still experience quite a fantastic life full of joy. If you genuinely want to live your best life, there are just a few more topics to cover. The next topic we want to discuss is the last 4 Ms: Meditation.

CHAPTER 15: MANIFESTATION

Now we get the final M of the 4, Ms. The one everyone loves to hear about...Manifestation. Yes, this is the feel-good part of the entire process. This is where we start believing in all possibilities, and it's a much lighter topic to discuss than our own personal issues and problems that we will need to work through first. The important thing at first is to come up with as many details about that dream life and, more importantly, who that person is within that dream. That person is you, but it's not who you are now. Otherwise, you'd be living the dream. So, how is that person? What do they think? What do they feel like? What do they act like? How do they treat people? How do they treat themself? Do they let their ego hold them back from success? No, they don't let their ego hold them back. Build this picture of what you want out of life as detailed as possible, as we discussed in the "Finding Your Passion" chapter. And then construct the kind of person you'd like to become. The kind of person you believe lives in that dream world. The kind of person that is your best self who lives their best life.

Now, spend some time honestly assessing your current self. "How am I different from that person living my dream?" Start drawing lines between that person's personality and your own. Break those goals into small steps or small goals. And start walking the path. Now that you have a map, you can start walking directly toward your goals instead of wandering aimlessly. Something Joe Dispenza says is to "feel like you already have what you want." This phrase may seem delusional at first to most, and we know it did for us in the beginning. Because we'd think, "I want to be rich," and then check our bank account, and we were still broke. We could feel good by imagining being rich, but then when we let reality set in by checking our bank account, we'd feel a lack again and feel like we were being delusional. It's more than just thinking. You have to combine that thought with a feeling (elevated emotions of relief, gratitude, joy, etc.) and then start acting on that thought and feeling. Start changing your habits into the habits that the future you have. Some of us were able to start getting a nice happy feeling just from thinking about a beautiful dream or possibility like becoming rich. This was a start, but we have to keep that feeling going throughout our day, not just when we're meditating on our dreams or daydreaming about our dreams. By continuously inspiring positive thoughts and emotions, we can more easily take action to pursue those dreams. These new positive thoughts, emotions, and actions are changing us within, changing the reality around us. As above, so below. As within, so without. It starts with changing yourself. Become the person who is worthy of those dreams you want. Your old self has to die for you to experience a new reality and live a new, better life. The techniques we've discussed in this book are all ways to slowly leave your old self in the past and move beyond your fears, doubts, and problems into your new self and your new best life. The beauty of this transformation is that it never has to stop. We can always think better, feel better, do better, act better, and be better. Once you accomplish one goal in your life, there's always another one you can begin trying to accomplish. Be curious about what you can achieve, and let that fuel your improvement.

Manifesting is more about having CERTAINTY that your dreams will come true. And how can you be certain that they'll come true? Start walking the path towards them and never let yourself, someone else, or any life situation stop you from walking that path directly towards your goal. It's like ordering your dream on WISH. You know it's coming; you don't know when. It could be here in two days or two months. Doesn't matter, it's coming. So stop checking the mailbox every 5 minutes. Get back to work; become the person who is worthy of receiving that gift and living that dream. You can't live that dream as the person you are now.

Change yourself so you can change your life. Start feeling great all the time. Stop letting your ego tell you that you can't do something. Start doing what you need to do to accomplish your dreams. You're going to fail along the way. You can't have success without failure; it just doesn't happen. So embrace the failure. It's a new lesson to learn, so you can give it a better shot next time. "Wow, getting closer now, but just a few more things to figure out." Eventually, you'll figure it out, get it right, and succeed. If we let fear of failure hold us back, then what was the point of starting in the first place? Now, we just wasted time making mistakes that were moving us toward our goal, but we let a few mistakes make us feel like a failure, so we quit our dreams. DON'T QUIT YOUR DAYDREAM! No dream would have been successful if that dreamer let themselves or someone else talk them out of making that dream happen. So, manifesting isn't about imagining a beautiful future. It's connecting that thought or imagination to the feeling you would have when it came true and then using that positive thought and emotion to take positive action to begin walking toward your goal. You can't just meditate all day and expect a million-dollar check to arrive in the mail. It's not going to happen. You haven't changed. You haven't suddenly become someone who deserved a million-dollar check in their mailbox. Don't wish for a lottery ticket; become the lottery ticket. Become the person who can make great money because they have the courage and the dedication to go out and accomplish that.

So we have to get off our butts! Start thinking, feeling, and acting like the person we want to be. Start holding ourselves to that new standard of our best self. Are we going to be that person instantly? No, but we look back on our day each night with an evening meditation or our thoughts and think of where we did well and poorly. We don't have to beat ourselves up for the bad; we can mentally rehearse what we could have done better and do that better thing next time. Then, in the morning, we can listen to a morning meditation, think to ourselves, and visualize our day. How can we make the best out of the day? How can we make the most progress at becoming the person we want to be? Never lose sight of who you want to become. Feel amazing now because YOU KNOW you will accomplish your dream because you won't let anything or anyone stand in your way. That gives you the confidence to start doing what you need to do, think what you need to think, and start FEELING how you need to feel. Feel amazing, why? Because your wildest dreams are going to come true, why? Because you're going to make it happen one way or another. Now, you can relax and enjoy the process, the path, and life's journey. Stop and smell the roses a bit. Isn't life beautiful? Yea, it is when you know your dreams will come true!

We want to use an example of someone finding their dream job and being worried about it. Fearing that they're not good enough for this job and letting that hold them back from obtaining this dream job. You have to let go and let the universe show you the way. If this is the dream job you've been waiting for and you get it, why stress about it? And if you don't get it, you must have a better opportunity. Maybe not immediately, but it will all happen in due time if you let it. That doesn't mean sitting around and meditating all day, expecting that just dreaming a dream makes a dream come true. You have to become the person who lives the dream. Who is that person? What do they do differently than you do right now? Do they wake up earlier? Do they work out? Do they make the best of each moment and not let their own self-doubts hold them back? Do they love themself? Do they show care and love to others when and wherever possible? What's the difference between you and the person you want to be? Make that distinction clear and hold yourself to that standard. No, you're not going to instantly be that person, but it won't take long if you make a list and decide to start doing everything on that list because why not? That's who you want to be, right? And who's holding you back from being that person? Only you. What's holding you back from living your dream? Not becoming that person. So, who's holding you back from your dream? It's just you. And it doesn't have to be. Flip the switch. Realize we have complete control of our lives, and there are no excuses. We have the potential to be great, or we have the potential to whine and tell ourselves, "It's too hard to change; I can't do that." You tell that part of yourself to kick rocks! You're too busy chasing your dreams to listen to that voice anymore. DON'T QUIT YOUR DAYDREAM! Be your best self, and your dreams will find you. Use that energy to manifest it when you speak to that employer next. Feel confident that this is YOUR JOB already. And if they decide to take someone else, it's just their loss, and you'll find another fantastic job that will see your potential and appreciate you. We know that whole saying "things happen for a reason" can seem like some "WooWoo" crap, but recognize that if they don't appreciate you now, they probably wouldn't have it later either, so you're dodging a bullet. Or they appreciate you; this is precisely where you're supposed to be. Either way, you win! You have something to be happy about. So stop worrying about it and be your best self. Be confident and show everyone that confidence. People aren't going to want to hire an unconfident person for a big job with many responsibilities. Unconfident people get the grunt jobs because there aren't as many responsibilities in that job description. Why would we ask an employer to have faith in our abilities if we don't have faith in our abilities? Let your manifestation give you confidence in achieving your goals. Let it be the reason you end up achieving them.

Next, we'll cover some manifestation techniques stated by several teachers and help you combine them so that your manifestations become as powerful as possible.

Harnessing the Power of 369 for Manifestation:
- Nikola Tesla, a pioneer in understanding vibrations and universal energies, placed profound importance on the numbers 3, 6, and 9. According to Tesla, these numbers held transformative creative energy capable of turning abstract ideas into tangible realities as a bridge between the intangible and the visible.

Unleashing Infinite Potential:
- In the vast universe filled with infinite potential, numbers play a mysterious yet influential role. The numbers 3, 6, and 9, particularly 369, are believed to possess significant potency, acting as keys to unlock boundless potential. Although the reasons behind their power may not be fully understood, the simplicity of their application makes them accessible to everyone.

The 369 Manifestation Method:
- Tesla's 369 method involves writing down positive affirmations three times in the morning, six times at midday, and nine times in the evening. Affirmations, concise statements expressing desires in the present tense, reinforce the idea that one already possesses what is sought. Phrasing affirmations with "I am" or "I have" invokes positivity, while phrases like "I will" or "I want" can hinder the mindset.

How to Use the 369 Method:
- To implement the 369 method, choose a clear intention, create a strong affirmation, and write it down three times in the morning, six times during the day, and nine times before bedtime. Visualization of desires is encouraged, coupled with a genuine feeling of joy and positivity.

Personalizing the Method:
- Creating a daily ritual using pen and paper adds a personal touch to the practice. This physical writing solidifies intentions in the mind and the universe's eyes, demonstrating commitment and determination.

Water Glass Technique:
- For a more time-intensive yet effective technique, try the "glass of water method." Jot down affirmations, place a glass of water on them, read the affirmations aloud, and drink the water. This method is rooted in the belief that water listens, as demonstrated by the experiments of Japanese businessman Masaru Emoto.

Additional Tips:
- The 369 method doesn't require waking up at 3 am, and the numbers are not related to time; they indicate the number of repetitions.
- Avoid forcing yourself if you're feeling grumpy or negative; this method is more effective when approached with positive emotions.
- Miracles may not happen overnight; success is about the energy projected into the universe and the emotions felt.
In conclusion, the 369 manifestation method, inspired by Nikola Tesla's insights, is a simple yet powerful tool to unlock the potential within and align oneself with the universe's vibrations. The key lies in consistency, positive emotions, and a genuine belief in the transformational power of affirmations. Next, we will reveal Joe Dispenza's manifestation techniques.

Joe Dispenza's Manifestation Method:
- Before delving into the transformative meditation guided by Joe Dispenza, it's essential to lay the groundwork for the potential experiences you seek to manifest. This preparation involves crystallizing your intentions, which requires translating your aspirations onto paper. Keep in mind that within the quantum field, all possibilities already exist, awaiting your awareness and alignment.

Symbolizing Your Vision:
Kickstart your manifestation journey by selecting a novel experience you aim to draw into your life. Assign this desired outcome a capital letter, considering it a symbolic representation of your reality. Enclose the chosen letter with two lines illustrating the electrical field (thought/brain) and the magnetic field (feeling/heart) you will generate around yourself. Think of this as aligning your energy with the potential inherent in the quantum field.

Detailing Conditions:
Take the process further by listing the specific conditions for this newfound reality. These conditions imbue the chosen letter with a more profound meaning and contribute to a heightened clarity of Intention. Exclude any mention of timeframes, focusing instead on the essence of your desires. For instance, if your aspiration is a fulfilling career, conditions include professional autonomy, collaboration with brilliant minds, impactful work, flexible remote options, and frequent travel.

Elevated Emotions Catalog:
- Construct a catalog of elevated emotions that will accompany realizing your intended reality. Begin with gratitude, a potent emotion associated with manifestation, often experienced after attaining a goal. Elevated emotions linked to realizing your aspirations could include empowerment, boundlessness, gratitude, freedom, awe, love for life, worthiness, and joy.

Guiding Principles:
- Cultivate an intimate familiarity with the energy associated with your envisioned reality. Ensure that external circumstances wield no power to divert you from your newly established state of being.

Recognition of Synchronicities:
- Anticipate the emergence of synchronicities in your life – these may manifest as serendipitous events, opportunities, or meaningful coincidences. Such occurrences signify your synchronization with new energy, and they naturally gravitate toward you without the need for active pursuit.

Tuning into Frequency:
- Envision this process as tuning into a specific frequency and then harnessing the powerful energy of your heart to draw your intended experiences into reality. As you embark on this transformative journey guided by Joe Dispenza, remain attuned to the boundless potential within your grasp, acknowledging your innate capacity to manifest your desired reality.

Putting it all together:
- If you want to manifest love, use the letter L, for example. L is a symbol that represents a potential new experience. So, draw the letter L and and circle it. Draw squiggly lines around it to express quantum energy and manifest this love from the universe. On the left side, write Intention. This means the thoughts of what you want to manifest. So please list what you want out of a partner and out of a loving relationship. Assign specific conditions of the relationship you would like. On the right side, write Elevated Emotion. This represents the feelings of what you want to manifest and how you would feel if and when this manifestation happened. Assign specific emotions you would feel when the experience occurred. By combining these two elements and keeping this in mind throughout your day, you can change your energy daily to draw this new life to you.

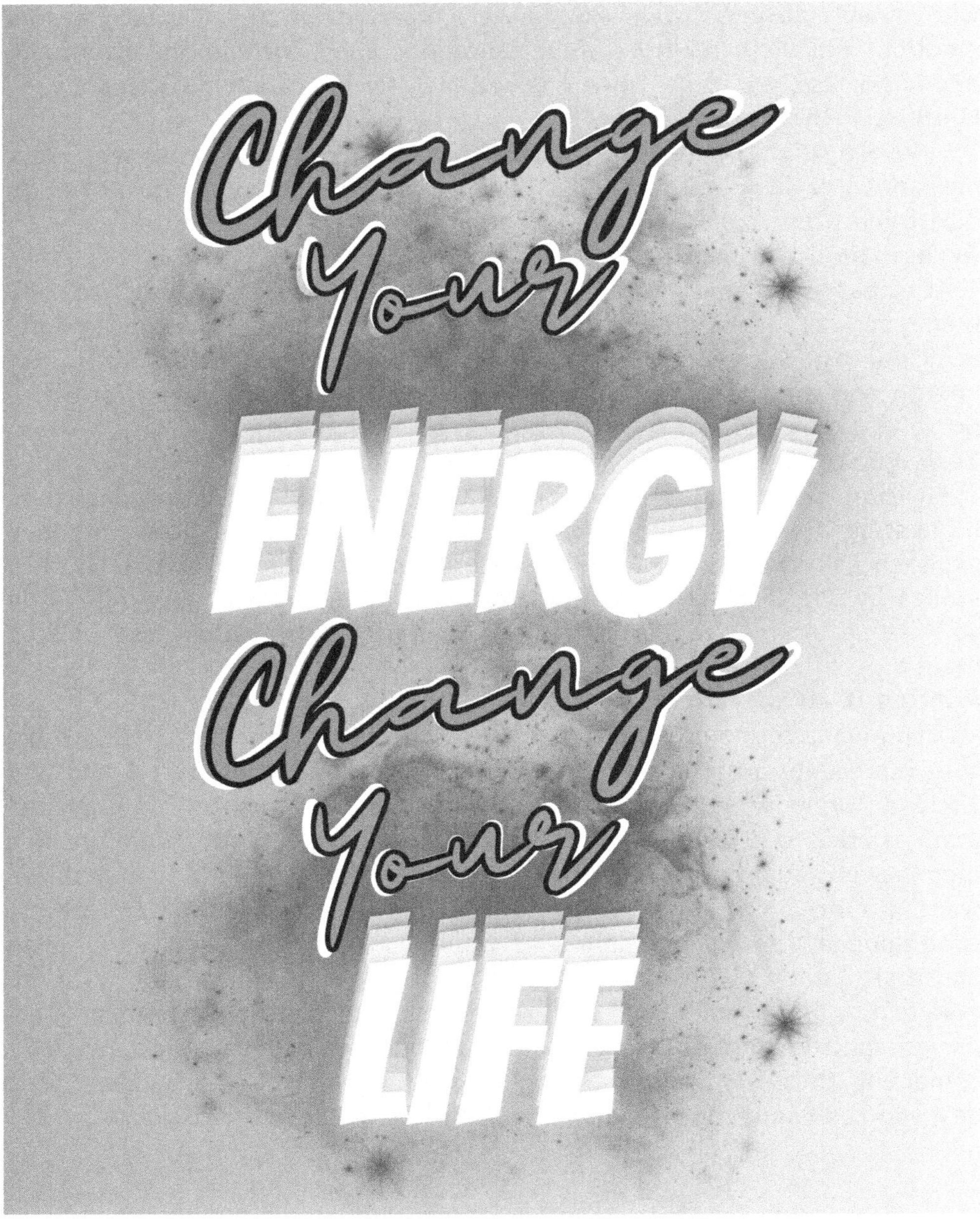
Change Your
ENERGY
Change Your
LIFE

Other Manifestation Methods:

Law of Attraction:
- Originating from the New Thought movement, the Law of Attraction suggests that like attracts like. You can draw positive experiences into your life by maintaining positive thoughts and feelings. Affirmations, visualization, and gratitude practices are vital components.

Vision Boards:
- This technique visually represents your goals and desires by assembling images, affirmations, and symbols on a board. Regularly immersing yourself in this visual aid helps reinforce your intentions.

Scripting:
- Writing a script or a detailed narrative of your desired reality can be a powerful manifestation tool. By vividly describing your goals as if they have already happened, you engage your subconscious mind and align your energy with your aspirations.

Meditation and Mindfulness:
- Ancient practices like meditation and mindfulness cultivate a focused and present state of mind. By quieting the mental chatter and promoting a sense of calm, these practices create space for intentional thoughts and desires to take root.

Crystal Manifestation:
- Crystals have been used for centuries for their energetic properties. Some believe that specific crystals resonate with particular intentions. Incorporating crystals into your manifestation practice, such as carrying them or placing them in your environment, is thought to amplify your intentions.

Feng Shui:
- An ancient Chinese practice, Feng Shui involves arranging your environment to promote positive energy flow (chi). You can enhance the manifestation process by aligning your space with your goals.

Affirmation Mantras:
- Drawing from Hindu and Buddhist traditions, affirmations and mantras are used to reprogram the mind and align with specific intentions. Repetition of positive affirmations can create a vibrational match with your desires.

Rituals and Ceremonies:
- Various cultures incorporate rituals and ceremonies into manifestation practices. Whether lighting candles, performing specific movements, or engaging in symbolic acts, these rituals can anchor intentions in the physical world.

Energy Healing:
- Modalities like Reiki and Quantum Healing involve channeling and directing energy to bring healing and manifestation. By addressing energetic blockages, practitioners believe they can facilitate the manifestation of desires.

Numerology:
- Drawing on the mystical properties of numbers, numerology assigns significance to numbers and their vibrations. Creating intentions aligned with specific numerological patterns is thought to enhance manifestation.

Creating Your Personalized Toolkit:
- Embrace the diversity of these manifestation techniques and experiment with what resonates most with you. Combining practices or tailoring them to your unique preferences can amplify their effectiveness. Remember that consistency and belief in the process are fundamental to successful manifestation. As you explore these techniques, trust in your innate ability to manifest your dreams into reality.

Mind Movies:
- Compile a video or a series of images representing your goals, dreams, and desires. Include affirmations, empowering music, and inspiring visuals that evoke the emotions associated with achieving your aspirations. Watching your Mind Movie regularly helps align your subconscious mind with your conscious intentions, reinforcing the belief in your ability to manifest your dreams.

Gratitude Journaling:
- Keeping a gratitude journal involves regularly expressing thanks for the positive aspects of your life. Focusing on gratitude raises your vibrational frequency, attracting more positive experiences.

Moon Manifestation:
- Harnessing the energy of lunar cycles, Moon Manifestation involves setting intentions during specific moon phases. New moons are often associated with new beginnings, while full moons symbolize abundance and fruition.

Sound Healing:
- Sound has transformative qualities, and practices like sound baths or using specific frequencies in meditation are believed to harmonize the mind and body, supporting manifestation.

Solfeggio Frequencies:
- Solfeggio frequencies are a set of ancient musical tones believed to have healing properties. Solfeggio frequencies for each of our energy centers, starting with 396 for the 1st center and going up to 963 for the 7th center. Incorporating these frequencies into meditation or visualization is thought to enhance manifestation.

Mirror Work:
- Popularized by Louise Hay, mirror work involves affirming positive statements while looking at yourself in the mirror. This practice fosters self-love and reinforces positive self-perception.

Akashic Records Exploration:
- Accessing the Akashic Records, a purported cosmic database of information, through meditation or visualization, can provide insights and guidance for manifesting your desires.

Lucid Dreaming:
- This involves becoming aware of a dream. Practitioners use this state to visualize and experience their desired realities, influencing the subconscious mind.

Biocentrism:
- Stemming from quantum physics, biocentrism posits that consciousness creates reality. By understanding and aligning with your consciousness, you can shape your experiences.

Sacred Geometry:
- Exploring sacred geometric patterns and symbols is believed to tap into universal energies. Integrating these symbols into your manifestation practice can amplify intentions.

Having certainty in your dreams and manifestations is the key. You're not delusional, telling yourself you have something you don't. You're just channeling the same elevated emotions you'd feel for that dream to be accurate, as if it's already happened. Or as if it's going to happen without a doubt. "The only limit to our realization of tomorrow will be our doubts of today." -Franklin D Roosevelt. This is basically how psychics end up having a placebo effect on people. If we told you that we could see your future and told you to guess what that future holds, what would you want it to be? And then our answer as the psychic to your perfectly described excellent future life would be, "Yes, that's exactly what's going to happen!" That's what's going on. But we're telling ourselves it will happen because it can and will as long as we keep feeling it's achievable and precisely what will happen.

Negative manifestations also work, and that's what we're used to doing. "Oh, I'm not good enough for that job, but I'll go to the interview anyway." What happens? You failed the interview because you never gave yourself a chance. People don't want to place real responsibility in the hands of someone who isn't confident. So, of course, you manifested not getting that job. There was no other possibility. Before the interview, you decided you weren't good enough for the job. You can do the same thing by thinking you are good enough for the job and good enough for any dream you want to manifest. This is how achievements happen. If any great achiever ever let anyone, including themself, get in the way of their dream and make them lose hope, then the achievement would have never been accomplished. They would have killed their dream, and they're the only ones who can do that. No one else can kill that drive, that passion, that dream. It's only us that can do it to ourselves. When we realize we can kill our dreams or support them, we free ourselves from the chains that have held us back this whole time—shame, guilt, unworthiness, fear, etc. So don't kill your dreams. DON'T QUIT YOUR DAY DREAM!

One last thing to keep in mind while you're manifesting. This may be the most important of all to add to your tool belt because no matter how well you positively manifest things, your old negative beliefs are still manifesting negativity in your life until you can leave them behind long enough that you're no longer affected by the negative manifestations you manifested weeks or months ago. This reiterates and restates the law of cause and effect, as discussed in Chapter 2. Here is a breakdown of this technique called the echo effect and how to understand it so you don't fall back into your old limiting/negative beliefs.

The Echo Effect – Thoughts Become Things:

- The echo of our thoughts reverberates through the fabric of reality, shaping the experiences that unfold in our lives. This phenomenon, often called the "Echo Effect," is a fundamental principle that transcends time, echoed in the wisdom of visionaries such as Napoleon Hill, Buddha, Gandhi, and Henry Ford. This relates back to The Law Of Attraction

The Power of Thought:

- Napoleon Hill, in his timeless work "Think and Grow Rich," illuminates the profound truth that a person is the product of their thoughts. This idea echoes through the teachings of spiritual leaders like Buddha and Gandhi, emphasizing that what we think, we become. Henry Ford's insight reinforces this, highlighting that our beliefs have the power to shape our reality

Thoughts Become Things:
- The Echo Effect operates on the principle that thoughts evolve into emotions, triggering actions that, in turn, manifest results in the external world. Every success story and innovation is a testament to the transformative power of this process.

Vibrational Frequency:
- Our entire being vibrates with a specific frequency, and this vibrational energy is broadcast into the world. Others receive this frequency, responding with synchronicities that align with our thoughts and emotions. This interconnectedness underscores the reality that our internal state influences the external world.

The Delay and Manifestation:
- Fortunately, there is a delay between thoughts, emotions, and actions, preventing instantaneous manifestation. This delay is a blessing, considering the complexities of life. If manifestation occurred immediately, the world would be chaotic. This delay provides an opportunity for us to course-correct and refine our thoughts.

Transition and Testing:
- As we transition from old limiting beliefs to new positive ones, the old beliefs may persist in our experiences. These are tests—a chance to prove our loyalty to the new belief system. Recognizing that these manifestations are remnants of the past and staying steadfast in the new belief is crucial.

Staying Loyal to the New Belief:
- Maintaining loyalty to the new belief involves resisting the temptation to revert to old habits and beliefs when faced with challenges. Rather than succumbing to the familiar refrain of "I knew it," focus on reinforcing the positive belief. Look for evidence that supports the new belief, believe in the invisible until it becomes visible, and let time play its role.

Facing Challenges and Embracing Growth:
- Challenges are blessings in disguise, providing opportunities to strengthen the commitment to the new belief. Faced with manifestations of old beliefs, it becomes a pivotal moment of decision—stay loyal to growth or regress to the familiar.

Enduring the Transition:
- Living in the old world created by past thinking persists until we endure the new belief long enough for it to transform our reality. This journey requires resilience, patience, and unwavering faith. Holding on to the new belief and letting go of the old paves the way for a profound shift in our world.

The Echo Effect is a dynamic interplay between thoughts and reality, allowing us to craft a life guided by positive beliefs and sustained growth. It is a journey of endurance, transformation, and the unwavering conviction that thoughts become things. So remember that those old beliefs manifested negativity to come in your near future, and those have to manifest. Stay true to the new beliefs through the turmoil you will face from the negative manifestations you created earlier. It's like the ordering from the WISH example we gave earlier. You ordered some bad news before, so it's still going to arrive at some point over the next few weeks and months. See them as packages that finally arrived, even though they're not the packages you want now. Accept them with grace and continue ordering positive manifestations from WISH. As long as you don't keep ordering negativity from WISH, your packages will soon enough be only positive things you ordered/manifested. Weather the storm, stay true to your new positive beliefs, and don't let the harmful packages you get in the mail affect your new positive beliefs. Keep ordering the positive gifts and paying attention to the positive synchronicities coming your way. Those negative gifts will stop coming soon enough.

It is all possible. The only thing holding you back is your belief in it. You can't heal if you don't believe you can heal. It sounds like a Snapple quote or something silly, but that's precisely how it works, and it has been proven with science and data. Others have preached the same things for centuries without having the science to back it up, just the evidence in their own life. You have to become a new person to experience a new reality. How you think, feel, and act has to change, or nothing will. Think you can heal, feel great about that thought, and act as if you're healing (not necessarily as if you're already healed; that will feel delusional).

Believing you are healing and will heal in time gives you the same feeling you would have as if you were already healed. It's all about your energy. Keep it elevated; keep feeling love, joy, relief, and gratitude; you will produce the right hormones to heal yourself. Practice tuning into your heart at all times. Keep an eye on it and the energy within your body. Feel the vibration at all times, and when you want to increase that frequency or vibration, then pay more attention to your body and your heart and think of gratitude, love, and forgiveness. Thinking positive makes you feel positive. Feeling positive makes you think positively.

Which side do you start with? Well, they work in tandem. So, begin with positive thoughts or start with positive feelings. You will get the other in return. Take positive action in your new life with those new thoughts and emotions. Begin chasing your dreams and finding what makes you happy so you can keep riding that comfortable train all day. We don't have to wait for things to change for us to change and feel great. We can feel great now and think great now so that something in our life begins changing and becoming more significant than before. Change your personality so that you can change your reality. If you keep waiting for your diabetes to be gone to feel great, it'll never heal. You have to feel great now, love yourself, and love life. And by doing so, the diabetes will subside. It was created through stress. It can only be healed by feeling no stress, the opposite of anxiety. You can do it; people have overcome many more incredible things by believing they could. It's not delusional; it's just how energy works. And we are energy, and so is everything around us. Start seeing everything as energy, and you will uncover the universe's secrets (Tesla). Manifesting becomes nearly instant once you eliminate the limiting beliefs in your subconscious, which the ego expresses. You start seeing synchronicities within every moment of life.

Anything you try to manifest out of fear or scarcity must eventually bring you pain at some point. So you do your best to manifest out of positive belief instead of fear or lack. Still, until we rewire our subconscious, the ego will sabotage other parts of our lives even when certain parts have been positively manifested. Who we are is already happiness and joy, except we don't know it. We don't know it because we haven't explored the false sense of self, which we call the ego. It's too caught up in judgment, acquiring things, fear, etc., and it will keep sabotaging us until we release those limiting/negative beliefs. If we found out who we are, the soul, then we'd have no use for the ego, and that's why the go keeps trying to hold us back. It needs to feel needed by us, the observer/soul. The ego becomes the barrier to inner purpose, peace, joy, love, and enlightenment (the top of the conscious transformation chart).

Mind movies or vision boards, too. I like having my phone wallpaper as something that also represents my dreams. Make sure you're not vague about your dreams, either. If you're wishing for money, have a dollar amount. If you're wishing for a partner, have their characteristics laid out. If you want a career, specify everything about it. The universe needs specifics; otherwise, it will give you a mixed bag, and the more you waiver back and forth between believing it's going to happen and not believing it will, the more the universe will be unsure of what you desire.

It's like ordering a hamburger and just saying you want a hamburger. The person taking your order must know what toppings, how you want it cooked, what condiments, etc. Otherwise, you'll get a plain hamburger and be upset about it. And when you go back and forth between believing in that dream, it's like you're telling your waiter, "I want a hamburger with lettuce, tomato, ketchup, mustard, cooked medium.....actually, nevermind I'm not that hungry.....wait, wait, yea yea I do want that hamburger.....well how are the burgers actually? Mmmm.....neh ill pass.....wait yea I'll take my original order please." You're gonna make that waiter quit their job

Be certain you can accomplish your dream because you've decided you won't let anything stop you from achieving it. No setback, no negative opinions from others, no speed bumps, no detours will ever stop you from achieving that dream. And because you're so CERTAIN of this dream coming true, you can feel amazing now about that dream coming true one day. That's how you feel like a champion, a creator, a master of your own life and universe. Certainty

Also, if you were certain you were about to receive the exact burger you wanted, you wouldn't run to the kitchen and ask the cooks how long it would take or make sure they got it right. You'd trust the process and sit back and enjoy the wait.

CHAPTER 16: WALKING THE PATH

In this chapter, we want to talk about the challenges we face within ourselves and especially from those around us as we begin to cross the river of change and head toward the path of becoming our best selves. Each time you feel something like guilt that lowers your energy, realize that it's taking you off the path, which means whatever thinking is lowering your energy has an untrue limiting belief behind it. So when you feel that way, start questioning whatever negative thought is present in your mind that you're having difficulty overcoming. If you have a friend or family member who doesn't seem to understand this new spiritual path you are taking, you may have negative thoughts about their attitude. "They are not spiritual at all" can be challenged by the opposite thought. So, ask yourself why the opposite is true. Why is "they are spiritual" true? Well, let's see...even if someone doesn't believe in God or an afterlife, it doesn't mean they aren't or haven't ever been spiritual. Many of the people we have quoted in this book are lovely for non-spiritual people to listen to because their research is based on scientific evidence and not so much from a religious standpoint. So if your friend or family members have a belief system that helps them be a good person, then that's great! And if they don't, you can only try to explain it a bit to them. It's not your job to show them the way; it's okay if you don't. That may be another phrase that makes you feel guilty. "It's my job to help my parents become more spiritual." And that makes you feel guilty, so where's the flaw? There must be a flaw because it's sending you into a primal state of fight/flight. So how is "it's not my job to help my parents become more spiritual" more accurate than the opposite? We feel that's a pretty easy one to decipher.

Even something like "my parents shouldn't be non-spiritual" is centered on this same negative belief. So why should they be non-spiritual? Well, they were probably raised non-spiritually, or something in their lives convinced them not to be spiritual. So, of course, they shouldn't be spiritual; it only makes sense. Understand that beliefs (including your parents) aren't necessarily rooted in truths, especially if they're negative beliefs causing negative feelings and thoughts within us. Our thoughts and feelings aren't our authority; they're just there to express the subconscious beliefs we have gathered through our own experiences. And understand that we're bothering ourselves and creating our own problems. Whatever the problem is, generally, it isn't an actual problem if we look at it objectively. We are making it an issue by allowing a negative belief to distort our reality.

Let's revisit the stand-up comedy example. Most of the crowd laughs, but a few people always decide to take offense to a joke. It wasn't a hurtful joke objectively, but it triggered a negative belief those people had within them. They let those beliefs distort their reality into negative feelings and thoughts. The problem isn't the joke. The problem is the negative beliefs within the people who took offense. Does that make them dumb, stupid, or wrong? No, their feelings are valid, just as all feelings are. But just because our feelings are valid doesn't mean they are truths that are best for us or that there's no better feeling we could attach to each situation. So ask yourself what negative thoughts keep coming up when you feel guilty around your parents or friends. What are those thoughts saying? And how are the opposite thoughts more valid than the ones that come up when you feel triggered with guilt? In the future, whenever you feel negative and hear some negative narratives in your mind, pause and ask yourself this: "Am I in danger right now? Is this fight/flight response the one I need in this situation? Am I being attacked? Am I being mugged?" If yes, then protect yourself and run. If no, figure out the opposite belief by figuring out the opposite thought and why it's more accurate than the one you're narrating that got you to this fight/flight state of being.

If you're having difficulty figuring out the opposite, give the mind a break for a second and go to your heart. Your heart will give you elevated emotions when you feel it, sense it, pay attention to it, and place your energy within it. So, if you can't find elevated thoughts at the moment (which will trigger elevated emotions), start the process with feelings by going to the heart. The heart will find elevated emotions, and then you'll think elevated thoughts. Either works; they lead you back to the positive path and state of being.

A final thought on this issue with your parents or friends: you can explain that water exists, you can show them where it is, and you can lead them to the water, but you can't make them drink it. And that's it. We can influence people, but we can't make them change. And there's a fine line between a gentle guide and an overbearing, forceful guide. Most people won't appreciate feeling forced or pushed into something. So be a gentle guide or decide they're not ready or willing to hear it, and that's okay, too. Notice these challenges as lessons for yourself to learn and keep the mantra, "This is exactly what I needed," in mind while facing adversity so you can see the silver lining. It was an opportunity to grow and a lesson you needed to learn.

Indeed, you can't change someone, but you can keep leading by example and influence them. You can show them the water and lead them to it, but their free will decides whether or not to drink it. We never want to be the person who decides to withhold the water from anyone, nor do we have to judge them for not drinking it. We can keep showing them the water, where it's at, and how to get there. We don't want to spam them with a map to the water, though. Some people aren't going to be interested in bettering themselves. When someone crosses our path again, we can show them the map. If they decide to crumble the map, that's fine; we won't pull out another map and keep showing them. But if they ever get curious and decide to see that map again, we're happy to pull it out and show them where the water is located and how to get there. We won't say, "Well, you crumbled the map, so why should I show you again!?" Resentment is only poison for ourselves.

We don't have to run from the fire of negativity now. We can see the fire and attempt to put it out. Remember that we can't put out every fire, but we can try. And we feel it's our duty as people who know where the water is to show those on fire where it is and that it exists. With great power comes great responsibility. That doesn't mean we'll let ourselves become overburdened by this responsibility, nor will we get so close to the fire and stay in the fire that it burns us, but we will not run from the fire in fear that it will burn us because we are firefighters now, and therefore we are safe from being burned. Same for our inner struggles of negativity. If we fear our trauma and our negativity, then we will only suppress it. We must face, accept, forgive, and then release it through the heart. Otherwise, it'll keep returning and strengthen each time it returns because we suppressed it. Everyone has the chance and the ability to evolve positively, and we can try to help some, but we can't help everyone.

Another thing to keep in mind is that you may begin slacking off and falling back into your old habits. This can be combatted in several ways. Suppose you have enough determination, willpower, inspiration, etc.. In that case, you can stay on the path without help from outside sources or other people. It will help to have a group of people or at least one accountability partner to help you stay motivated and on course. Sometimes, you only need a pat on the back or words of encouragement. If that's not enough for you either, you may need to implement consequences like money or punishment if you don't stick to your goals. You can pay a friend some money and tell them they get to keep it if you still need to accomplish your goal by a specific date and time. You can also pay to join a group that empowers each other. So when you want to slack off or give up, the cash you've already spent on the group can motivate you not to quit. This is why paying for a gym membership can help some people, but it only helps some. Figure out what works for you, and feel free to ask for help. Asking for help isn't a weakness, as most of us believe. Here is a comprehensive list of strategies we just mentioned, as well as other ideas to help you stay on track when you start to fall back into old habits:

Overcoming Setbacks:

Mindfulness and Awareness:
- Encourage regular self-reflection and mindfulness practices. Awareness of one's thoughts, emotions, and behaviors is crucial for recognizing when old habits resurface.

Set Realistic Goals:
- Break down long-term goals into smaller, achievable steps. This makes the transformation journey less overwhelming and helps individuals stay motivated with tangible progress.

Accountability Partners:
- Suggest partnering with a friend, family member, or mentor who can support, encourage, and hold them accountable. Sharing the journey with someone else adds a social element and strengthens commitment.

Celebrate Small Wins:
- Acknowledge and celebrate every small success. Positive reinforcement boosts motivation and helps individuals focus on their achievements rather than perceived failures.

Adaptability:
- Emphasize the importance of flexibility and adaptability. Life is dynamic, and setbacks are inevitable. Adjusting goals and strategies in response to challenges is critical to long-term success.

Positive Affirmations:
- Encourage the use of positive affirmations. Remind individuals to replace negative self-talk with affirmations reinforcing their capabilities and the positive aspects of their journey.

Learn from Setbacks:
- Instead of viewing setbacks as failures, help individuals see them as opportunities for learning and growth. Ask questions like, "What can you learn from this experience?" or "How can you adjust your approach moving forward?"

Create a Supportive Environment:
- Assess the individual's environment and identify potential triggers for old habits. Please encourage them to make adjustments or seek support to create an environment that fosters positive change.

Establish Consistent Routines:
- Routine and structure can provide stability during times of change. Help individuals establish consistent daily habits that align with their transformation goals.

Professional Guidance:
- Recommend seeking guidance from therapists, coaches, or counselors. These experts can offer personalized strategies and tools to address specific challenges.

Visualization:
- Guide individuals to visualize their desired outcomes. Creating a clear mental image of success can be a powerful motivator and keep them focused on the end goal.

Reconnect with Purpose:
- Remind individuals of their initial motivations for embarking on the self-transformation journey. Reconnecting with their purpose can reignite passion and commitment.

Self-Compassion:
- Encourage self-compassion during difficult times. Remind individuals that setbacks don't define them, and treating themselves with kindness is crucial for maintaining resilience.

Community Engagement:
- Engage in communities that share similar transformation goals. Connecting with others facing similar challenges can provide a sense of belonging and shared experiences.

Continuous Learning:
- Emphasize the importance of continuous learning and personal development. Encourage individuals to explore new information, skills, or practices that align with their transformation journey.

We want to include a quick guide to adding nutrition and exercise into your life as you progress and transform into your best self. There isn't a perfect diet or exercise routine for you. You have to try out different things and customize your own. We each have a foreign body and, therefore, will hardly ever fit perfectly into a generalized workout or exercise plan. Find what works for you and enjoy the journey of trial and error.

Personalized Nutrition and Workouts:

Nutrition: Your Unique Fuel:
- Recognize that nutrition is a deeply personal aspect of your well-being. No single diet works for everyone due to bio-individuality. Consider the following steps:

Experiment:
- Try different diets (e.g., Mediterranean, plant-based, paleo) to understand how your body responds.
Allergies and Sensitivities:
- Identify any allergies or sensitivities by gradually reintroducing foods and noting reactions.
Cultural Preferences:
- Acknowledge and respect your cultural food preferences, ensuring your diet aligns with your heritage.
Observation:
- Keep a food journal to track how certain foods impact your energy levels, mood, and overall well-being.
Listening to Your Body's Signals:
- Developing a mindful eating practice enhances your awareness of your body's nutritional needs
Hunger and Fullness:
- Listen to your body's hunger and fullness cues. Eat when hungry and stop when satisfied.
Food Awareness:
- Be mindful of the sensory experience of eating. Notice textures, flavors, and how different foods make you feel.
Emotional Eating:
- Distinguish between physical hunger and emotional triggers for eating. Address emotional needs without relying solely on food.
Intuitive Eating:
- Allow yourself to choose foods that align with your body's needs intuitively.

Workouts (Embrace Your Unique Fitness Journey):
- Just like nutrition, workouts aren't one size fits all. Consider these steps:

Discovering Your Preferred Activities:
- Exercise should be enjoyable to maintain long-term commitment. Explore various activities to find what resonates with you:
Diverse Options:
- Experiment with dancing, hiking, swimming, weightlifting, yoga, or team sports.
Fun Factor:
- Choose workouts that bring joy and fulfillment. If you enjoy the activity, you're more likely to stay consistent.
Social Engagement:
- Consider social aspects; join classes or groups that share your fitness interests.
Building Consistency and Progress:
- Establishing a consistent workout routine is critical to long-term success
Start Gradually:
- Begin with manageable workouts, gradually increasing intensity and duration to prevent burnout or injury.
Goal Setting:
- Set realistic fitness goals, whether they're related to strength, flexibility, endurance, or a specific activity.
Progress Tracking:
- Keep track of your achievements and celebrate milestones. This can boost motivation and reinforce positive habits.
Adaptability:
- Be attuned to your body's signals. If you experience fatigue or discomfort, adjust your routine accordingly.
Rest and Recovery:
- Allow time for rest and recovery. Adequate sleep and rest days are crucial for overall well-being.

By recognizing the uniqueness of your body's responses to nutrition and workouts, you empower yourself to create a sustainable and fulfilling health journey. The key is to stay open to experimentation, listen to your body, and embrace the joy of movement and nourishment in a way that aligns with your individual needs and preferences. We also want to include techniques people use to combine mind, body, and spiritual growth. These practices focus on holistic well-being, combining physical movement, breathwork, and mindfulness. Here are some examples:

Holistic Practices:

Yoga:
- **Focus:** Mind-body connection, flexibility, strength, and spiritual awareness.
- **Characteristics:** Various styles, including Hatha, Vinyasa, and Kundalini, with a focus on poses, breath control, and meditation.

Tai Chi:
- **Focus:** Martial art promotes balance, flexibility, and relaxation.
- **Characteristics:** Slow, flowing movements, deep breathing, and meditation, fostering harmony between mind and body.

Pilates:
- **Focus:** Core strength, flexibility, and overall body awareness.
- **Characteristics:** Controlled movements, precise breathing, and an emphasis on the core muscles.

Martial Arts:
- **Focus:** Self-discipline, physical fitness, and self-defense.
- **Characteristics:** Various styles with specific movements, stances, and forms.

Aikido:
- **Focus:** Martial art centered on self-defense and redirecting an opponent's energy.
- **Characteristics:** Circular and flowing movements, promoting harmony and non-resistance.

Capoeira:
- **Focus:** Brazilian martial art combining dance, acrobatics, and music elements.
- **Characteristics:** Fluid, rhythmic movements, often performed playfully and interactively.

Feldenkrais Method:
- **Focus:** Improving body awareness and movement efficiency.
- **Characteristics:** Gentle, mindful movements to explore and improve physical function.

Alexander Technique:
- **Focus:** Improving posture, movement, and coordination.
- **Characteristics:** Mindful exploration of body alignment and movements.
Gyrotonic Expansion System:
- **Focus:** Fluid movements to increase flexibility, strength, and coordination.
- **Characteristics:** Circular and spiraling motions using specialized equipment.

Qi Gong:
- Focus: Similar to Tai Chi, emphasizing energy cultivation and balance.
- Characteristics: Slow, intentional movements, coordinated with breathwork.

MELT Method:
- **Focus:** Self-myofascial release and improving body awareness.
- **Characteristics:** Use specialized soft rollers and small balls to release tension and improve alignment.

Ballet:
- **Focus:** Artistic dance form with benefits for flexibility, strength, and posture.
- **Characteristics:** Graceful and precise movements, often performed to music.

Somatics (e.g., Hanna Somatics):
- **Focus:** Mind-body integration, releasing chronic muscle tension.
- **Characteristics:** Slow and mindful movements, promoting awareness of internal sensations.

Dance (Various Styles):
- **Focus:** Artistic expression, cardiovascular fitness, and coordination.
- **Characteristics:** Diverse styles include contemporary, jazz, hip-hop, and more.

These practices offer a range of options for individuals seeking a mind-body approach to health and well-being. Choosing the one that resonates most with personal preferences and goals can contribute to a holistic and enjoyable wellness journey. Next, we will discuss how to develop positive relationships in your life. We will include a list of things you can do to cultivate positive relationships.

Creating Positive Relationships:

Building Meaningful Connections:
- Building and nurturing positive relationships is a fundamental aspect of personal well-being. Healthy connections contribute to emotional resilience and support during challenging times and enhance the overall quality of life.

Effective Communication:

- Effective communication forms the cornerstone of any meaningful relationship. It involves more than just speaking and listening; it requires a deep understanding of each other's perspectives. Here are some essential aspects of effective communication:

Active Listening:
- Cultivate the habit of genuinely listening to others. Give your full attention, maintain eye contact, and refrain from interrupting. Respond thoughtfully to demonstrate that you value what the other person is saying.

Expressing Yourself Clearly:
- Articulate your thoughts, feelings, and needs clearly. Be honest and open without imposing judgments. Clarity promotes mutual understanding and fosters trust.

Non-Verbal Communication:
- Pay attention to non-verbal cues such as body language, facial expressions, and tone of voice. These elements convey emotions and nuances that words alone may not capture.

Feedback and Validation:
- Provide constructive feedback and validate the feelings of others. Acknowledge their experiences and express empathy.

Empathy and Understanding:

- Empathy is the ability to understand and share the feelings of another. Cultivating empathy enhances the depth of your connections with others:

Perspective-Taking:
- Put yourself in the other person's shoes. Consider their experiences, emotions, and worldviews. This helps create a sense of mutual understanding.

Validation:
- Acknowledge the emotions and experiences of others, even if they differ from your own. Validation fosters a supportive and non-judgmental environment.

Empathetic Responses:
- Respond to others with empathy. Offer support, encouragement, or simply a listening ear. Demonstrating empathy strengthens the emotional bond in relationships.

Setting Healthy Boundaries:

- Healthy relationships strike a balance between independence and interdependence. It's crucial to maintain individuality while fostering a connection with others:

Personal Space:
- Respect the need for personal space and time. Allow yourself and others the freedom to pursue individual interests and hobbies.

Shared Activities:
- Engage in activities that you both enjoy. Shared experiences strengthen bonds and create lasting memories.

Effective Collaboration:
- Collaborate on decisions and plans, considering the input of each person involved. This collaborative approach fosters a sense of partnership.

Recognizing Toxic Relationships:

- Not all relationships contribute positively to your well-being. It's essential to recognize signs of toxicity and take appropriate actions:

Identifying Red Flags:
- Be aware of behaviors such as manipulation, excessive control, or constant negativity. These may indicate a toxic relationship.

Setting Limits:
- Establish clear boundaries to protect your well-being. Communicate your limits and be prepared to enforce them if necessary.

Seeking Support:
- If you find yourself in a toxic relationship, seek support from friends, family, or professionals. Surround yourself with those who uplift and empower you.

Cultivating positive relationships is an ongoing process that requires mindfulness, communication, and a commitment to mutual growth. Building meaningful connections and setting healthy boundaries create a fulfilling and supportive social landscape. Now, we will list ways to embrace the challenges that come your way along this path and how you can see that even the lower moments of our lives are meant to be something to learn from.

Embracing Challenges and Growth:

- Life is a journey filled with challenges and opportunities for growth. This chapter will delve into the importance of resilience, adaptability, continuous learning, and personal development as integral components of navigating life's ever-changing landscape.

Resilience and Adaptability:

- Resilience is the ability to bounce back from adversity, and setbacks are an inherent part of the human experience. Here's how to cultivate resilience in the face of challenges:

Mindset Shift:
- Adopt a growth mindset that views challenges as opportunities for learning and improvement. Embrace setbacks as stepping stones toward personal evolution.
Reflection:
- When faced with a setback, take time for self-reflection. Understand the factors contributing to the challenge and identify lessons to be learned.
Positive Self-Talk:
- Develop a habit of positive self-talk. Encourage yourself with affirmations reinforcing your ability to overcome obstacles and emerge stronger.

Embracing Change and Uncertainty:

- Change is constant, and uncertainty is inevitable. Embracing these aspects of life allows for personal growth:

Flexibility:
- Cultivate flexibility in your thinking and actions. Embrace the idea that change often brings new opportunities and experiences.
Mindfulness:
- Practice mindfulness to stay present in the face of uncertainty. Focus on what you can control and let go of the need to predict or control every outcome.
Adaptability:
- Develop adaptability as a core skill. This involves adjusting your approach, strategies, and mindset to navigate evolving circumstances.

Continuous Learning and Personal Development:

- The pursuit of knowledge and personal development is a lifelong journey. Here's how to foster a mindset of constant learning:

Curiosity:
- Cultivate curiosity about the world around you. Ask questions, seek new experiences, and remain open to discovering new ideas and perspectives.
Reading Habit:
- Develop a habit of reading regularly. Explore diverse genres, from fiction to non-fiction, to expand your understanding of various subjects.
Online Courses and Workshops:
- Leverage the wealth of online courses and workshops available. Platforms like Coursera, Udemy, and Khan Academy offer opportunities to acquire new skills and knowledge.

Expanding Skills and Knowledge:
- Personal development involves not only acquiring knowledge but also honing practical skills. Consider the following:

Skill Assessment:
- Identify areas where you'd like to improve or acquire new skills. This might be related to your career, hobbies, or personal interests.
Goal Setting:
- Set specific goals for skill development. Break down larger goals into manageable steps and celebrate milestones along the way.
Networking:
- Engage with online and offline communities that align with your interests. Networking provides opportunities for shared learning and skill exchange.

Embracing challenges and committing to continuous learning and personal development empower you to lead a fulfilling and meaningful life. Through resilience, adaptability, and a dedication to lifelong learning, you navigate challenges successfully and evolve into the best version of yourself. Remember, the path of self-transformation is a marathon, not a sprint. It's a stairway to heaven, not an elevator. Fostering a supportive and understanding environment that promotes resilience and growth is essential. This means you may need to let go of or distance yourself from negative people, even if they're family or close friends. Some of those family members or close friends may want to join you on this journey, and that's wonderful.

Some people you know may already be on this path and will welcome you. However, those who want to pull you off that path or create more stress and negativity in your life must be kept at a distance or wholly cut off for you to succeed. "The only people who get upset when you set boundaries are those who benefit from you not having any." Carlos Dominguez. It's not an easy decision, but when you make that kind of decision, you will know it's right and won't regret it. You can offer advice or a helping hand to those people, but most need more time to be ready to transform their lives like you are. You can only show them the map of water. Let them know it exists, show them the way, and lead by example, but you can not make them drink!

CHAPTER 17: TIME TRAVEL

Okay, let's not get our hopes too high because of the title. We haven't created a time machine...yet. Still, we can technically time travel within our minds, and we do it naturally every day. We've all relived the past by thinking back to a situation. Doing so, we end up feeling like we did back then. We may feel nostalgia, guilt, shame, grief, etc. But just by revisiting our past through memories, we can experience that past situation as if it is happening to us now. Our body feels the same effects; our mind thinks the way it did back then, and we may even act on that memory now that we are feeling like we are reliving it.

We've all also dreamed about a possible future at some point. Maybe that dream came true; perhaps it didn't. We still felt like that dream was real while we dreamed it in our sleep or during our waking days. These daydreams are just possibilities that our mind comes up with. Night dreams tend to be our subconscious trying to tell us something important, so paying attention and writing down our dreams is good. Some daydreams we relate to, and that may decide that we want it bad enough to go out and make it happen. Our night dreams of horrible possibilities that we don't want to happen. We can use that as a guide to help us avoid those awful possibilities or learn the lesson these nightmares are trying to portray. We can fear our dreams, or we can embrace them.

The beauty of "time traveling" to the future is that the future isn't set in stone. We can search our mind for any possibility we want and begin latching on to it and manifesting it anytime. Once we have that dream or that goal in mind, we can start breaking that goal into small steps. We inevitably walk a direct path toward that reality as we take those small steps. If we no longer want that dream, maybe it wasn't for us. Or if we decide we're incapable of that dream, it will die. We will stop walking the path toward that dream, so it will only be possible if we start walking that path toward that dream again. As we become more in tune with that future reality that we want, we begin seeing synchronicities. These are proof that we're getting closer and closer to our goals. Things start unfolding for us positively, revealing more of the path we can continue to walk towards that dream. We also can see and receive more explicit images of that dream we want by tuning into that reality more often. It becomes more and more specific as we decide more and more that it will happen. So, simple random thoughts we used to have begun dissipating, and all we tend to see now are visions of the future. When your dreams become apparent, you can more effectively and efficiently "time travel" to the future and gain some insight from that reality.

Many artists have claimed to have received their creations in a dream. Stephen King, JK Rowling, Martin Luther King Jr, etc. These dreams didn't appear to them out of nowhere. They had their heart set on accomplishing a goal, and they were able to tune in to all of the possibilities surrounding that goal. Some images they received may not have fit what they were looking for. Others are precisely what they want, and they can't explain how they thought it up. It's almost as if their future self presented them with a gift from the future. Who's to say that this didn't happen?

Time is not linear, and we know that now. Just as we know, the Earth is not the center of the universe, and that matter is made up of energy. Linear time is an artificial invention to obtain organization within humanity. And because we look at time as linear, we don't see the possibility of time travel. We don't understand that our minds can view the past, present, and future anytime. It depends on where you place your awareness, energy, and consciousness.

The perception of time by the soul, unbound by the linear constraints we experience in the physical realm, opens a philosophical exploration into destiny and free will. While the soul may have a broader understanding of the events that will unfold, it doesn't necessarily imply a fixed, predetermined fate. With its timeless perspective, the soul might recognize potential paths and outcomes. Yet, it retains the capacity for choice and redirection. Consider the soul as a navigator with a map that shows various routes. It sees the paths laid out before it, acknowledging the possibilities each one holds. However, the journey is flexible. The soul possesses the agency to choose a different route, explore uncharted territories, and redefine its course based on its choices. In essence, the non-linear perception of time by the soul doesn't eliminate free will. Instead, it offers a vantage point that transcends our limited understanding of the past, present, and future. The soul may have insights into the potential of its journey. Still, the dynamic nature of existence allows for continuous adaptation and redirection. So, while the soul might glimpse the threads of its destiny, the tapestry it weaves is a collaborative effort between its timeless wisdom and the choices it makes in the present moment. The unfolding of the soul's journey remains a dance between destiny and free will, a dance where it can pivot and pirouette in new directions at any moment it discovers its true north.

Emotions affect time and space as well. Emotions change our reality. Emotions add spice to our lives. Emotions are how we remember things. Connecting an emotion to an event burns into your mind, and you remember it forever. This explains why women tend to remember more than men. They feel emotions more readily throughout the day than men so that they can recall full events and details. In contrast, men remember the basics and will soon forget those basic details because there's nothing memorable about them. We may retain some non-emotional experiences we had earlier that week. Still, those non-emotional experiences will be erased from our minds soon enough.

The mind doesn't see the point in remembering things that did not create an emotion within us. There are too many more important things the mind holds onto. It doesn't want to fill up its memory drive with useless memories. This is why, as we get older, we feel like life is speeding up and passing us by. We become more and more detached from our emotions. Because we've seen it, we've done it, we've lived it. Life becomes the same boring routine, so it has no meaning, and there are no emotions attached to the things you do throughout your day. Therefore, time feels like it's flying by, and when you look back to just a few days or even a week ago, you realize you hardly remember any of it. Why? Because it could have been more memorable. Now, here's the thing about unique experiences. They can be anything. They don't have to be excited to remember; they must carry an emotion. Any emotion will do. Think about any memory of your past. The first thing you remember is how you felt at that time. That feeling you remember then helps you relive the reality you were living back then, now in the present, both mentally and physically. It's time travel. If you were feeling great, you filled in the memory gaps with how you imagined things would have played out based on your mindset (a happy one). Of course, some things don't have gaps; we remember what took place because we recognize how we felt and what we did due to feeling that way.

Therefore, if you want time to stop flying by, stay present in the moment and start enjoying life. Start adding emotions and feelings to the things you do or your life in general. If you decided to enjoy doing the dishes for the first time today, you'd remember that experience. "Yeah, I was dancing and singing along to my favorite song. I even got so carried away with dancing that I broke a glass on the floor, but I cleaned it up quickly and didn't let it bother me." That simple task is now embedded into your memory. So you see, we don't have to wait for fun events to start feeling emotions and clinging to those moments as a source of enjoyment. We can feel joy right now and place it into everything we do by feeling our heart, sensing it, and involving it in the present moment.

Time will start to slow down. We will begin to remember most things we do daily because they finally have meaning. And our reality will shape around us based on how we feel. If we feel great and something misfortunate happens, we tend not to think negatively about it. We deal with that misfortune and get back on the horse. It doesn't have to destroy our joyful reality and send us to a new negative reality where everything is doom and gloom. There's no hope, and life sucks, and we can't do anything right. No, we can keep that joyful feeling going and see things positively. We will remember most of those events if we attach negative feelings to everything. Time will slow down similarly, but now time is slowing down, becoming a reality of hell instead. Most people don't realize how emotions and beliefs make up our reality. Once we recognize this and understand that we have control over our beliefs and feelings, we know that we have control over our entire reality and life. There are things we can't control, but we realize that and don't place any worry on those things because there's nothing we can do about them. At that point, why would we choose to live in hell on Earth when we have the option to live in heaven on Earth? Why not then choose heaven on Earth every time?

CHAPTER 18: TRUST THE PROCESS

We want to break down the techniques we discussed into a shorter summary to help you remember what we covered earlier in the book. We can look back on this summary for quick assistance or guidance. You could use this as a detailed summary for someone interested in living their best life or a quick recap for the book when you want to reflect and remind yourself of the things you learned.

1. Start Meditating

- Try it without guidance. Guidance will help you build the skills you can develop by meditating, but let's start by focusing on what's going on with our mind and body when we slow down and shut out the rest of the world. No distractions; it's just you and your thoughts. Just close your eyes and be still, then wait to hear what the mind and body want to say. Become aware of those thoughts and feelings. They are your autopilot, and they are resisting this new change. Your autopilot will try to convince you to stop this new activity, not because your body and mind naturally want to sabotage you from growth but because they want things to stay the same. The body and the mind want to run the same programs all the time, so life is a seamless flow. Change is difficult for the body and mind, and we must first understand that we must forgive our body and mind for making this change process more difficult. We also want to address the possibility that some people may hear testimonials of people healing from doing a meditation and think, "Oh wow, all I have to do is listen to this meditation, and then BOOM, I'll be healthy again?! Well, let's put one on right now!" Meditation is not the end-all-be-all of this work. It is only the beginning. Meditation is training wheels. Meditation helps you become aware of yourself. This helps us see that we are not the body or the mind. We are the soul, the observer, and the witness of what our body and mind are doing and communicating to us. We are the consciousness that hears, sees, and experiences what is happening inside and outside the body and mind. We are the link between the physical world and the quantum world. Our body and mind are not our authority; they make up the vessel that helps us experience this physical world.

2. Become Self-Aware

- You can begin deciphering the code written into your subconscious autopilot by listening to your thoughts, which will narrate how the body feels. Your mind and body may say, "I don't want to sit still; this is dumb. I don't like it. Here are some stress hormones. I know you like them. What else must I do to get you to stop this new action? Hey, remember that time you were upset with your parents? Look, here's that time your ex broke up with you. Can we stop this now, or do you want us to keep thinking about your worst traumas?" By paying attention to these narratives, you can start breaking down what subconscious belief each thought is expressing. The first belief that was brought up in this hypothetical narrative was, "I don't like change." You do like change; change is how we grow. Your autopilot doesn't like change; there's a difference. The second belief was "I enjoy being stressed." You don't enjoy being stressed; you're body and mind are used to feeling stress though, so it feels normal to you. The example about your parents may be some belief like "my parents don't care about my feelings" or "my parents don't want what's best for me." The situation about your ex may be concerning your self-worth and self-esteem or a fear of abandonment.

3. Become Mindful And Stay Present

- This is the action of becoming self-aware. It's a significant part of changing your beliefs and your reality. Being mindful is having a constant awareness of your habits and programs. It's easy to turn off your awareness and let the body and mind keep doing what they're used to. Listening to and noticing what your mind and body are trying to communicate can be challenging. Some things we're used to noticing, like being hungry. We know what that generally feels like, so it's easy to connect that feeling of hunger to the message that the body is hungry. The mind helps fill in the blanks with a narrative attached to it anyway. It'll say, "Wow, did you feel that rumble in the stomach? Must be hungry." We tend to overlook other communications because they're not as important to us as hunger; that's a survival instinct, so it needs to be voiced loud and clear, or we won't survive. A thought or belief like, "I can't do that. I could never do that. That's way too difficult" can be overlooked and not challenged. This is a negative belief we let slip through our conscious awareness of ourselves.

Being present and mindful is continuously being aware of those thoughts and challenging them with logic, reason, and the opposite belief. It doesn't need to be challenged if it's a positive belief, but we also want to be aware of and reinforce it. We also may have been overlooking thoughts and beliefs about life, the world, and the people around us. "Wow, I can't stand that person! They're a jerk!" Are they, though? You've never seen one instance of them not being a jerk? If your answer is no, you've probably not paid enough attention to them and seen the good within them. Are they the issue here, or is the issue that we allow someone or something in our outside world to affect our inside world? Here's the thing about jerks: it's rather hard for them to keep being jerks if they're not getting a rise out of you and you're not throwing negativity back at them to fuel their own negative fire.

Ignoring them is a quick fix and can work in the long run, but embracing them positively is an even more effective way to deal with negative people. Of course, you have to set up boundaries. You don't want to overextend your kindness to the point that you are hurting yourself, but either way, you want to let it go. You'll see much better results and usually quicker than avoiding or ignoring them. The same thing works for the bully within our minds. The more we ignore and suppress negative emotions and beliefs, the more they build up. Instead, we want to forgive bullies in the outside world and our inside world. Don't let them bother us, at least, and practice forgiveness. Forgiveness helps us release that negative energy so we can focus on other things and not be constantly reminded about those negative things. By forgiving, we free ourselves from the burden.

4. Change Your Beliefs

- By recognizing the deep-rooted beliefs beneath the narratives of our mind, we can start understanding our subconscious beliefs and then work on changing those beliefs. "I'm not worthy" can become "I'm worthy." However, we must first find those beliefs before changing them. You may already know some of these beliefs but have chosen not to change or didn't know you could change. Beliefs shape the way we think, act, and feel. Our personality is the way we think, act, and feel. And our personality shapes our personal reality. So, by changing our beliefs, we inevitably change our personality and personal reality. Think about any belief you have. Often, people think of religion when they hear the word beliefs, and that's one of the most significant beliefs that shape us.

If you can recall when you first started becoming religious or maybe decided to become non-religious, then you can recall how much this changed how you thought of, viewed, and experienced the world. You began tying God to it all. "What would God think? What would God do? Look what God made! This thing must have happened because God wanted it to." And the opposite happens when you dismiss God from your beliefs. Maybe your parents raised you in religion, so thinking back to how you viewed the world before God was instilled into your mind may be difficult to remember, but we believe you can understand how it would change the way you view the world. This is a rather significant belief that shapes you, so it's easy to see, but what about more minor beliefs? What about a traumatic experience with some animal, maybe? If a dog bit you, or someone threw a lizard on you, or someone put mayonnaise in your hair, then you're gonna have a traumatic experience that shapes a new belief that dogs are mean, lizards are scary, and mayonnaise is disgusting. These minor beliefs won't shape every aspect of your life like religion can, but they will affect your life nonetheless.

You may view some of these negative beliefs as unimportant to change because they don't affect much in your life, but realize that even the smallest negative beliefs can hold us back. If you're afraid of dogs, you're going to let dogs affect your energy, and you're going to feel less connected to nature because fear will hold you back. If dogs or lizards are scary, why wouldn't other animals be considered scary? Animals are somewhat unpredictable, which can be unnerving, but if we fear them, we disconnect from them and nature. We no longer see the similarities we share with them. Instead, we focus on the differences and become detached. Animals are energy, just like us. They are living organisms, just like us. They are here to procreate and evolve just like us. We are also animals; we live pretty different lives than other animals because of our brain power. So now that you're aware of your beliefs, it's time to change the ones you realize no longer serve you well. How do we do that? Attach a new thought, action, and feeling to the old belief when it arises or when you force it to come up by thinking about it. "Okay, so I'm afraid of dogs. I choose to be no longer afraid of dogs. My new thought process is that dogs are not scary." Now, you have to associate an action of sorts. If there's a dog around, petting it would be a perfect action to retrain your beliefs. Face that fear and show your mind that it was wrong to assume the negative belief it has grown accustomed to. If a dog isn't present, imagine petting it and reacting well to your touch.

Lastly, we must attach an emotion to this new thought and action. Any elevated emotion will do: gratitude, relief, joy, love, etc. This new belief is burning into your memory because emotions tie events to our memory. Now, you have two conflicting beliefs in your subconscious. The more powerful belief of "dogs are scary," and the less powerful, new belief of "dogs aren't scary." Now, "dogs aren't scary" has a vote; it has a leg in the race. It may have already had a vote somewhere in your subconscious, but it was heavily outweighed by the countless votes that say, "Dogs are scary." What now? Well, either keep bringing this belief to the forefront of your mind and challenging it, or wait for it to present itself again and challenge it once again with your new belief (new thought, new action, new feeling). If you do this enough times, the new belief will have more votes and outweigh the old belief.

5. Practice Emotional Intelligence

- This is that forgiving part we just mentioned. Essentially, it's shadow work and getting in touch with your heart. How do we forgive? Once we've started getting a handle on being the observer of our own thoughts, we can begin challenging or analyzing those thoughts. But the other thing we want to do is forgive ourselves and other people for these negative beliefs and emotions. Holding resentment only poisons us. It's the metaphorical act of drinking poison, expecting to poison someone else, when, in turn, we are only poisoning ourselves. So, how do we forgive ourselves and others? With our hearts. If we focus on our heart and feel it and/or sense it, we will find elevated emotions. This energy center, where the heart resides, stores all our elevated emotions like forgiveness, love, gratitude, etc. So when we feel upset at something, someone, or ourselves, the best practice is to slow everything down. Take a breath and focus on your heart beating. Let it guide you towards more healthy thoughts and feelings. With this practice, we can begin releasing our negative energy and traumas. Just let it go. Understand that negative energy only keeps us from growing into our best selves.

6. Manifest What You Want In And From Life

- Manifestation involves envisioning a possible reality, not just imagining or visualizing it. Envisioning is imagining or visualizing PLUS feeling the emotions and the frequency of that possible reality. And then connecting to it so profoundly that your belief that it will happen becomes a certainty. If you knew your future, you wouldn't stress about how or when it would happen; you'd enjoy the ride and be happy to be on the journey towards that future you want. First, you must imagine that future and begin filling it with as many details as possible. Then you can start feeling what that future would be like. So, how would you feel if that possible reality you want to become your personal reality? We guarantee you will feel elevated emotions of gratitude, relief, joy, inspiration, love, wholeness, etc. So manifesting is imagining that reality and then feeling that reality as well. How would you act? How would you think? What would you do? Where would you go? Embody that reality. Become that person who lives in that reality, and that reality will begin to manifest. You have to change yourself to change your reality. Manifesting draws a direct line from who you are now and what you are experiencing to who you want to be and what you want to experience. By connecting to that reality and feeling, acting, and thinking like that person who lives in that reality you want, you are forcing that reality to become your own personal reality.

To start feeling confident about this skill, it's good to try some easier and simpler manifestations at first so that you can start getting the hang of it. Try manifesting small things like seeing your favorite animal, finding a specific coin somewhere strange, getting a good parking spot at the store, hitting all green lights in traffic, seeing a butterfly, finding a feather, getting a call or text from a friend, receiving smiles from strangers, etc. These are small, and you can chop them up to coincidence or see that by focusing on these possibilities, you open up your awareness to them, and they become synchronicities.

7. Practice Them All Together

- Once you've learned these individual skills, they can all come together into you, transforming your life through thought alone. You can stop letting things bother you, begin assessing and changing your negative beliefs into positive ones, embodying elevated emotions and thoughts, and connect to the future reality that you want for yourself. Meditation will help us practice these things without distraction. These skills we learn without distraction can be implemented throughout our day when distractions arise from all directions. We can learn to calm our minds and stay focused on becoming the person we want to be by focusing on how we think, act, and feel. Think positive, act positive, and feel positive; your reality will be centered on positive things. Don't forget that negativity exists. We don't want to ignore negativity or develop hatred or intolerance for it within ourselves or the outside world. We can learn how to deal with it, face it, accept it, forgive it, and let it go to return to focusing on positivity. Negativity doesn't have to rule your life, but it can if you don't acknowledge it and decide to shift it into positivity. You can't change what you're not aware of. We must awaken our soul to help lead us toward the positive path we want for ourselves. Become aware of the chains holding us back so we can detach them and not let them hold us back anymore. The chains of negative energy, thoughts, beliefs, perspectives, and mindset. Recognize them to release yourself from them, not ignore them and act like they aren't there.

Here is a summary of how to break free from the matrix of our mind and defeat the ego:

- The first place to start is becoming aware of your thoughts and feelings. Meditation helps us train that skill. We're emptying our minds of good and evil thoughts. When we're done meditating, we want to continue practicing that skill of self-awareness throughout the day. Be aware of how you feel. Reinforce the good thoughts and feelings and start recognizing the bad. Do your best to not react at first. Let those negative thoughts and feelings be there without forcing you to respond negatively. It's not easy, and you'll fail at first, but it's okay. As you get good at that, you may start feeling emotionless since you're suppressing it all and not letting it out. That's okay, too. It's just a start. You're learning to stop letting your emotions and feelings dictate your actions. The ego causes us to think negatively, making us feel negative, so we're learning to stop giving it authority and power over us. It was great for our growth in childhood, but now it's becoming our worst enemy, so we have to recognize it and stop letting it have power. The next step is having the courage to stand up to the ego and detect the falsehoods in the negative things it's saying. It's sending us into a primal state of fight/flight, and we're not in actual danger, so there's a lie or a falsehood in its narrative somewhere.

Now, we can start looking for the lie. If we can't find the lie, we can flip the narrative, find the opposite thought, and find truth in that opposite positive thought instead. There is always truth in the positive and always lies in the negative. So when you think "I can't," realize it's lying, look to the opposite, "I can." "Wait...I can. But how? How is that true?" Just by asking yourself that question, you open the door to possibilities. "Oh yeah, I can do it; I just have to learn how to do it, or stop focusing on a big impossible goal and start breaking it down into small achievable goals." It's the same when your ego says, "Well, I'm going to fail, and I don't want to be embarrassed by failing." Failure comes with success. You can't succeed without getting some things wrong first. It doesn't matter how much you study something; you'll need to practice it and fail it a few times to get good at it.

So embrace the mistakes and failures. See them as learning opportunities to do better next time. Be excited to be wrong when you're in a debate with someone. You can learn something. There's no room for growth if we close our minds and become ignorant. Opening our minds allows us to learn new things from people we may have never listened to because we have a closed mind. So, back to arguing with the ego. Once you've debated it once, you won't need to discuss with it again why you CAN do something. You'll hear "I can't" and think, "Oh well, that's a lie, and I already proved it, so no need to listen to that again." The last step is to learn how to forgive your ego and anyone who has hurt your ego. That's how we release that negative energy for good. It won't come back then because we hugged it and forgave it. Now, it can move on. Telling the ego it's wrong and to go away suppresses those negative feelings. Forgiving it with your heart will let it go.

You can start small and work your way up. It's not a race. Just try to do better each time. The problem isn't getting upset. It's allowing yourself to STAY upset. Did you let it ruin your whole day? Or an entire event? A full 5 minutes? You can do better next time; just be glad you finally got off the ground and back on the horse. Back on the happy train. Back to grace. How long will you let yourself fall from grace next time? Hopefully, it won't take long because it's not the moment that upsets us; it's us who bothered ourselves about it. Tell the ego to take a hike until you learn to forgive it. See the ego as the avatar or the character your soul is playing. This will help you create separation from it, control it, and forgive it for its outbursts.

If you feel that you are still carrying the weight of your traumas, then sit with yourself and let yourself feel those feelings that you keep avoiding and are afraid to touch. Bask in the presence of those uncomfortable emotions and let them flow. This heavy energy will cause you to cry it out. Embrace that cry, let the tears flow, and let yourself fully feel the emotions you've been suppressing. When you think you've cried out about as much as you can, switch gears to feeling forgiveness. Forgive those who hurt you in the past, and forgive yourself for holding on to these traumas and weighing yourself down this whole time. It often helps to voice your forgiveness to yourself and others during this practice. Then, metaphorically or literally, hug that trauma, those negative feelings, and that pain you've held inside for so long. Hug yourself and let that energy go by forgiving it. Feel that forgiveness in your heart as the negative power is released through your heart. Let those tears of sorrow turn into tears of joy. You will feel lighter and more full of love when you remove all that pent-up negative energy.

You've had love within you this whole time; it's just been covered up by that trauma and that pain. Once you release that pain, you will have more room for love. Your light will shine bright now that the smoke in the jar has cleared. Doing this just once should help you feel a massive change in your emotional state moving forward. Try this multiple times for the best results, slowly releasing all that pent-up negativity with forgiveness. Eventually, you won't have tears of sorrow left to cry, only tears of joy for being free and full of love.

One last shorter summary of what we teach in this book:

First, we must learn to stop reacting and begin thinking before responding. That creates awareness of the ego.

Second, we have to use that awareness to recognize the negative patterns of the ego. This begins separating us from the ego.

Third, we have to regain control over the ego by not taking any more abuse from it. We should not allow negative self-talk to lower our energy.

Fourth, once we have control over the ego, we can invite it back to examine what falsehoods lie within the negative/limiting beliefs and logically see that the opposite, positive thinking has more truth in it.

Fifth, we can release those negative beliefs through forgiveness. Forgive those who instilled those negative beliefs within us, and forgive ourselves for carrying the baggage that weighed us down for so long.

Sixth, when we have released most or all of that negatory energy and those negative beliefs, we now become the creators of our lives. We're free to manifest whatever we'd like. We cannot manifest what we'd like until we release those negative beliefs through forgiveness because we don't believe we're capable. This is the way.

So, with meditation and mindfulness, we can first learn to block out all thoughts to create separation.

Second, we can begin noticing the thoughts that keep coming up.

Third, we learn to specifically block out negative thoughts to gain control.

Fourth, we invite those negative thoughts back in to be examined.

Fifth, we see the falsehoods within them and rewire them into more truthful, positive thoughts.

Sixth, we forgive all and release. Then, we can manifest anything.

We hope this summary breaks things down into a clear and precise action plan for you. These teachings, techniques, and practices come together somehow; sometimes, we don't see how they connect. We want to shine a light on them all and show how they come together so that we aren't too focused on just one thing and expecting one piece of the puzzle to change our lives instantly. It's not just one thing, and it's not an instant change. It takes practice, dedication, and persistence to learn and achieve anything. This work is no different from learning to ride a bike, read a book, or play a sport. It takes time and effort to achieve results. There is no single fix-everything piece of the puzzle. It is a collection of the puzzle pieces and how they fit together. Trust the process and stop worrying about when or how results will happen. They will come in time and keep walking the path of enlightenment. Worrying about how and when results will come will only slow down the process because those thoughts are generated from lack and insecurity.

CHAPTER 19: FINAL LESSONS

We have to explain the final lessons that will help you live your best life. We saved the best lessons for last. The first is to follow what excites you. This idea is encapsulated in Bashar's Formula. Bashar's Formula concisely expresses his teachings, encapsulating critical principles of creating one's reality. The Formula is:

1. Follow your highest excitement every moment to the best of your ability without any insistence or assumption on the outcome.

2. Act on the opportunities that align with your excitement and fall within your integrity guidelines.

3. Stay open to the infinite possibilities in each moment and trust the timing of your reality, knowing that everything is unfolding perfectly.

Here is a more in-depth breakdown of this Formula:

Understanding Your Highest Excitement:

Self-Reflection:
- Take time for self-reflection to identify activities and experiences that genuinely excite you.
- Consider moments when you felt most alive, fulfilled, and passionate.
Explore Your Passions:
- Engage in activities that genuinely interest you. It could be a hobby, a form of creative expression, or any activity that brings you joy.
- Experiment with various activities to discover what truly excites you.

Applying The Formula:

Moment-to-Moment Awareness:
- Cultivate mindfulness to be present in each moment. This helps you recognize opportunities and your emotional response to them.

Tune into Your Feelings:
- Pay attention to your emotional responses. A sense of joy, enthusiasm, or curiosity often accompanies your excitement.

Decision-Making Process:
- When faced with a decision, consider the options available to you.
- Evaluate each option based on how aligned it is with your highest excitement.

Clarify Intentions:
- Clearly define your intentions for each decision. What outcome aligns with your highest excitement?

Detachment from Outcome:
- Detach from specific expectations or outcomes. Focus on the joy of the experience rather than being fixated on a particular result.

Examples And Insights:

Career Choices:
- When considering career options, explore industries or roles that interest you. Pursue a career that aligns with your passions rather than societal expectations.

Relationships:
- In relationships, choose partners who bring out the best in you and contribute to your personal growth. Follow the path that aligns with your values and desires.

Hobbies and Creativity:
- Dedicate time to hobbies or creative pursuits that excite you. This could be painting, writing, or any form of self-expression that brings you joy.

Educational Pursuits:
- When choosing educational paths, select subjects that interest and excite you. Learning becomes a joyful journey when aligned with your passions.

Travel and Exploration:
- Plan trips and experiences that resonate with your interests. Whether exploring nature, learning about different cultures, or pursuing adventure, choose what excites you.

In-Depth Insights:

Overcoming Fear:
- Recognize and overcome fears holding you back from following your highest excitement. Often, fear masks the path to your true desires.

Evolution of Desires:
- Understand that your highest excitement may evolve. Be open to shifts in interests and passions as you grow and explore.

Trusting the Process:
- Trust that following your highest excitement is a journey. Results may only sometimes be immediate, but the joy in the process is valuable.

Alignment with Core Values:
- Ensure that your decisions align with your core values. This ensures a sense of authenticity and fulfillment in your choices.

Collaboration with Others:
- Collaborate with like-minded individuals who share your excitement. This enhances the collective experience and creates a positive, synergistic environment.

Course Correction:
- Be open to course corrections. If a chosen path ceases to excite you, allow yourself the flexibility to adjust and select a new direction.

Following your highest excitement is a dynamic and personal journey. It requires self-awareness, openness to change, and a commitment to living authentically. Embracing this principle can lead to a passion, joy, and purpose-filled life. Essentially, follow excitement and happiness with every decision you make, but also keep in mind your beliefs. If you're at work and you know that the most exciting thing you could do is walk out on your job and chase your dreams, your beliefs tell you that it won't work out for you. If you're going to crash and burn, then wait to take that leap. Begin chasing your dreams while only working that job once you can support yourself without that job. In the meantime, choose the most exciting thing to do at work or the most exciting thing to say to your coworkers or boss. Keep the conversations fun, engaging, funny, etc. What's the funniest thing you're able to add to this conversation? What are you passionate about, and would you be excited to discuss it with the people around you? What are the people around you excited to talk about for hours? What's their passion? What excites you in your life currently? What thrills other people in their lives currently? Follow excitement at every moment. What is the most exciting thing you could do right now?

Do that until you can't do it anymore or until you feel like doing something else that would excite you more now that the excitement of that last choice has worn off. Again, apply reason and logic to this. Of course, we'd all like to spend tons of money traveling and doing enjoyable things, but not all of us can afford that. So what is the most exciting thing you can do now within reason? There are countless free or cheap options to find compelling. We're sure you even have plenty of exciting things you can do for free at home. Understand what excites you and begin doing those things as often as possible. The more you chase excitement, the more your life will start to unfold in unique ways. You'll begin recognizing incredible synchronicities and feel like life is quite magical. Things will fall into place for you, and it will seem like everything in your life happens for a reason, and you're so happy that it does. You'll begin to feel in awe of life itself. If you don't believe us, then give it an honest try. Do your best to chase excitement every moment for a few days and tell us you can't relate to the words we just wrote; we dare you! And what's the harm in trying? Chasing excitement keeps you looking at life with a glass-half-full mentality. It maintains a smile on your face and your energy elevated. It helps you feel gratitude and love for your life and existence. With enough practice of this technique, you'll feel like you're living a fairytale. You'll be living your best life.

At some point, you may feel so connected with the 5D/quantum realm that you start to lose touch with the 3D world. Some believe this is their need to "go home," but we'd like to assure you that you're already home. There is always more; ALWAYS. And it's always more of you. Your entire reality is you. So everywhere you shine the flashlight of consciousness, you find more of yourself. Keep shining it around, and don't be afraid of what you see. Hint: it's gonna be more of you. Fearing the unknown is simply fearing discovering more of ourselves. Home is to either become more of one with yourself or more of one with everyone else. Either way, more love and understanding are on that path toward "home." As soon as we feel we've got everything figured out, the universe has a way of showing us that we were silly ever to believe such a thing. Perhaps you're already home, and this feeling you're getting is that you don't know that about yourself yet. It's like chasing validation from others, which is an endless chase that never works out in the long run. If you seek validation from others, you give them the keys to self-esteem and happiness. Instead of wanting validation from other people for us to feel love for ourselves or to feel worthy or whole, the whole point is to learn that we were whole the entire time; it was just our limiting beliefs (other people's baggage) that made us feel like we weren't complete. Only other people's bags weigh us down.

We suggest you investigate why you don't feel like you're home already if you do. Perhaps you don't feel quite enough love or worthiness within you for yourself. Who knows? Only you!

The other final lesson we want to teach is about facing your fears, and it's verbatim, word for word, exactly what Bashar teaches about fear. We couldn't find a better way to express it, so we used his exact words. Bashar is amazing; please listen to as much of his content as possible. We may fear the unknown, but what do we think will be hiding and waiting to get us? Many of us fear our nightmares, but there's no need to. Nightmares can be exciting instead. What do we learn from them about ourselves? We learn what we fear and how we define our fears. That's a great thing. We allow those nightmares to transform into dreams by climbing on board that nightmare and riding it until it becomes Pegasus. A nightmare is a dark horse, and Pegasus is a flying horse. Get on and ride it until it transforms into a horse with wings that will soar into the clouds of your dreams. The polarity of Pegasus is that you must ride the nightmare first to ride Pegasus, though. The definition we have of the unknown is what is scaring most of us. The only thing that exists in the unknown and the only thing we will ever discover in the unknown is more of ourselves. That's all there is for you to discover in the unknown: more of you. Because you are your reality. You fill your reality up. There is nothing in your reality but you. So, even in the unknown parts of your reality, the only thing you will ever discover when you turn on the light is you. So ride the nightmare and find out what it's telling you. Find out what you're telling yourself. Learn from it. Grow from it. Invite it in, get on it, and ride it. Then it will transport you, and before you know it, you'll look down and sit on a bright white horse with a spread of wings soaring into the clouds. Because that's the polarity of Pegasus: You have to ride the nightmare to be able to ride Pegasus.

It's okay for you to be afraid, but the idea is that once you acknowledge that it's okay to be afraid, then you'll recognize what fear is. It's a messenger knocking on your door, saying, "Hey, I'm trying to get your attention here. I '"m trying to let you know that you have a belief system that's out of alignment with your true self." That's what fear is. You are a 100% energy. You feel your energy in different ways when you filter your energy through different belief systems. When you filter your energy and let it flow through belief systems that align with you, you feel it as joy. When you filter your energy through your belief systems that are out of alignment with your true self, then you feel it as fear. That's your barometer. That's what tells you, "Oh, I'm feeling fear. Well, that must mean that I have a belief system that's out of alignment with me that I don't prefer. Thank you, fear! Thank you for bringing that to my attention!" Fear will say, "Well, now that you've used the message as intended, see you later!" The fear doesn't hang around once you allow it to do its job of simply delivering the message of bringing your attention to something you want to know about. So don't blame little fear, poor little fear. Knock, knock, knock. "GO AWAY!" you say. Fear responds, "I'm just trying to deliver you a message." "No, Go Away," you say again. "Aw, I've been given this job to deliver messages to you, and you won't even open the door and let me deliver it." And then fear sulks away and says, "Okay, well, I'll show her. I'll come back even stronger!" Bang, Bang, Bang! "Oh my goodness, there's that fear again, and now it's even louder. Go away! I don't want anything to do with you!" "Let me in," fear says. "No, No, No, not by the hair of my chinny chin chin." "I'll huff, and I'll puff, and I'll blow your house down," fear says. And believe us, it will. Because you want it to come in. You want the message it has, and if it has to blow your house to smithereens to do it, then it will because you're telling it to do so. That's what you designed fear to do. So, the sooner you open the door, the better. Ding Dong. "Fear Here." "Oh, good day, fear. What piece of juicy information do you have about me today?" "Well, you have this belief system, you see? And it's out of alignment with you." "Oh, really?" "Oh, yes. Here, sign here, please." "Have a great day, fear. Please come back again as soon as you have any more information." "Don't worry, I will! I'm on the job!" And that's how you make a friend of fear and use it for the job it was designed to do so that it doesn't have to grow into a giant scary monster to get your attention. That's all it's attempting to do: get your attention. And believe us, it will get your attention when you force it to grow big enough. But you don't necessarily prefer to have your attention gotten in that way, so pay attention sooner.

You can start following excitement with every decision you make. In that case, you will continuously feel elevated emotions and immense joy in life. You will be following your guide the whole way. It will lead you to your dreams and your best life. Once you can stop letting the ego control you and begin forgiving the ego as well as everyone and everything, you will be able to feel confident about yourself and about living life to the fullest. You will no longer be afraid of having a bad day; it won't be left up to chance anymore. You will know you'll have another fantastic day because you make that choice when you open your eyes in the morning. You now have the tools to feel amazing in every moment not let negative emotions rule you, and keep you down. If you can also begin welcoming what's left of your negative energy, that negative energy left over will also be released quickly. We view our hearts as a jar of light. That negative energy clouds the light in the jar. The only way to remove that negativity is through forgiveness. Forgiveness is what opens that jar and allows the clouds of negativity to be released. Ignoring that negativity, fearing it, or trying to toughen it up or push through it will never work. We must embrace all parts of us, including those we disowned and feared to peek at long ago. That's inauthenticity and will cause us fear and stress, which is the opposite of living your best life. The key to living your best life is forgiveness and acceptance. The meaning of life is creation, so figure out what you'd like to create in this lifetime and start chasing that dream today, not tomorrow! Face your fears so they no longer own you. When you choose to disown a part of yourself, it holds you in return. The truth shall set you free, but it's going to piss you off first or at least hurt. It's worth it to go through the pain in the short term to escape the long-term pain, though. Keep your energy elevated and watch your mental and physical health rapidly become healthier than ever before. See all of these challenges in a positive light. Find this change journey exciting and won't be nearly as challenging to accomplish or overcome. It's all about how you look at things. See the glass half full, and your life will become full of wonder and surprises. Enjoy the ride towards living your best life, and make the best of each moment. See each moment as the exact thing you need to experience right now. Even the more challenging times can be seen as positives when we use this perspective. When you live like this, every moment becomes a synchronicity.

Remember when you start feeling like you need to do one of these steps correctly in this transformation journey: There's no wrong way. There are more efficient ways, but if you keep walking North in the dark, you'll find the North Pole one way or another. Your soul wants to thank you for just showing up. "80% of success is just showing up." -Woody Allen. We want to help people get there faster and take the direct route, but some things are more accessible to feel than to describe in words. You're feeling it already; you're growing. Keep showing up for yourself, and great things will happen; it's inevitable. Do well for you. Become your biggest cheerleader. We get one chance at this, as far as we know. Even if we do get multiple chances, this one matters!

We only have a short time here; we have to get going. It's time to be our best selves right now without delay. We must keep showing up for ourselves and start walking the path directly toward our wildest dreams. Know where we're going, at least, and what's different about our best self in that dream compared to the person we are today. We don't need to look at the past except to love where we came from and discover our mistakes so that we may turn them into lessons—mentally rehearsing what we'll try differently next time—accepting the challenge of learning more and growing and stepping into the unknown with a map for guidance. We know where we're going; we don't know what will happen. We'll be able to navigate better and quicken the walk on our path with wisdom from others who have walked a similar path before us. We will join hands with others who walk our current path to the same destination. We'll be forced to leave others behind who do not follow our path, which may sadden us. Still, times will come when others need to take the other side of the fork in the road, and we must wish them well and thank them for taking a walk with us. You will get to the North Pole one day, so stop and smell the roses. Enjoy the walk; it's a relatively peaceful and beautiful one. Any time we let fear and negativity guide us in the wrong direction, we can always forgive ourselves and return to the path towards True North. Knowing where True North is in the first place gives us the confidence to venture toward it. Otherwise, we'd wander in the dark, looking for something we cannot comprehend.

Having that map of True North gives you confidence in your walk, and may have that map allow you to feel joy, excitement, gratitude, love, relief, etc. Feel that way now; feel elevated emotions now because you'll feel that way later; you know it's coming! And that's the most immense comfort we could have in life. Show up for yourself and give yourself comfort. Stay present with yourself because you're living your daydream; this is the prequel of that daydream. DON'T QUIT YOUR DAYDREAM! Find Your True North and keep walking towards it no matter what happens. If you want to live your daydream, all you have to do is wake up and see that this is a dream in the first place. We're not from the 3D realm, we are energy, We are 99.99999% energy, which means we are quantum; everything is.

Our Final Message To Our Readers:

Ladies and gentlemen, seekers of knowledge, we will reveal the secrets of this life. Imagine a realm where the keys to the universe are not elusive mysteries but tangible truths waiting to be unveiled. Right now, we invite you to embark on a journey of discovery, where the brilliance of Nikola Tesla's enigmatic words becomes the guiding light to unlock the secrets of the cosmos. Tesla, a luminary ahead of his time, proclaimed, "If you only knew the magnificence of the 3, 6, and 9, then you would have the key to the universe." Let those numbers resonate within you, for they hold the potential to unravel the very fabric of existence. In mathematics, Tesla's 3, 6, and 9 are pillars of cosmic significance. Picture them not merely as numerical entities but as harmonies echoing through the corridors of creation. As we delve into the vibrational frequencies, we find parallels between these numbers and the mystical 369 associated with the root chakra.

Consider this convergence not as mere coincidence but as a celestial orchestra playing the cosmic symphony. The universe whispers to us through these numbers with mathematical precision, beckoning us to decipher its codes. In this quest for understanding, we are not merely seekers but pioneers of enlightenment. Each step we take towards comprehending the mathematical patterns woven into the fabric of reality brings us closer to the keys that open the gates to universal wisdom. As Tesla envisioned, these numerical wonders are not arbitrary; they are the cosmic glyphs that reveal the grand design. Imagine a world where the secrets of creation are not shrouded in obscurity but laid bare for those with the courage to explore.

By exploring 3, 6, and 9, we are decoding the mysteries of mathematics and resonating with the fundamental frequencies that connect us to the universe. The keys to the cosmos are not distant dreams; they are the very numbers that dance in harmony with the heartbeat of creation. As we journey together into the depths of understanding, let the spirit of inquiry guide us. With each revelation, we draw closer to a reality where the universe unfolds its wonders, and we stand as enlightened custodians of the keys to the cosmos.

Imagine this journey not as a whimsical adventure but as a profound exploration into the very essence of our being. The keys to the universe, often attributed to the mathematical wonders of 3, 6, and 9 by Nikola Tesla, resonate deeper than mere numbers. These keys, mysteriously linked to our root chakra and the awakening of Kundalini energy, hold the promise of liberation from the shackles of fear, greed, insecurity, materialism, and ungroundedness. In the sanctuary of our root chakra, Kundalini rests, an energy center susceptible to blockages that impede our physical and mental freedom, trapping us in the confines of the ego. The awakening of Kundalini isn't a complete detachment from the ego; instead, it's a realization that we are the eternal observers of the ego, participating in a 3D simulation called life.

As we free ourselves from these self-imposed constraints, we rediscover our origin in the quantum dimension. This awakening is remembering that we chose to play the game of life, experiencing time linearly and immersing ourselves in the profound mystery of existence. Our ancestors, perhaps aware of the quantum realm, concealed this truth to make the game more captivating. If we don't know we're playing a game, then that game becomes more immersive and believable. Acknowledging this reality may seem like disrupting a carefully crafted narrative, but it invites us to question the stressful world constructed by societal norms. We may be breaking up the party by revealing the veil placed over our eyes, but we believe we can create a much better party together. While stress teaches valuable lessons, there's an alternative path—happiness and peace. We can choose to feel love, collectively shaping Earth into an extraordinary place to dwell.

The journey involves transcending the negativity of the root chakra, liberating ourselves from ego-driven illusions, and returning to where we belong. Yet, the beauty lies in continuing to play the game with newfound awareness. The game, still enjoyable, unfolds as we choose happiness over stress and love over fear. It's a collective endeavor to transform the Earth into the incredible playground we envisioned. Embrace the journey, rediscover the quantum realm within, and let the game be one of joy and fulfillment.

Once we understand that we control this life, we can manifest anything. It's no longer a game of chance when we know we're all in this thing we call life together, creating this illusion of life without our 6th sense of energy. The pineal gland contains our soul/consciousness of self. And as it gets calcified by the illusion of ego and the 3D world, we become more and more detached from self. We've believed that we are stuck in this 3D world because those who do know and don't want to share this info with anyone are running society and freeing themselves, but enslaving the people within their own egos by affecting our emotions and causing us stress from society from birth. When we sense energy, we can sense ourselves, the soul/observer. "God" is within means that "We are within." We are within our ego, physical body, and mind. We are the creators of this life as quantum beings.

A Kundalini awakening is the act of freeing ourselves from the 1st energy center where the ego lies and freeing ourselves to the source/God/universal consciousness. 396 is the frequency of Kundalini/root chakra/1st energy center. Once we escape the constraints of the ego, we can begin embracing our heart center (639 frequency). Once we feel enough love inside, we can begin becoming enlightened and graduate to the crown chakra energy center (963 frequency). This is what awakening truly means: transcending your ego so that you may transform into higher levels of consciousness, thereby living life with high-frequency elevated emotions that vibrate so high that you can completely control your life. That is how you feel safety, relief, love, joy, peace, gratitude, purpose, and enlightenment. This is how you climb up the scale of consciousness.

Yet, the beauty lies in continuing to play the game with newfound awareness. The game, still enjoyable, unfolds as we choose happiness over stress love over fear. It's a collective endeavor to transform the Earth into the incredible playground we envisioned. Embrace the journey, rediscover the quantum realm within, and let the game be one of joy and fulfillment. Once we understand that we control this life, we can manifest anything. It's no longer a game of chance when we know we're all together, creating this illusion of life without our 6th sense of energy. When we sense energy, we can sense ourselves, the soul/observer. "God" is within means that "We are within." We are within our ego, physical body, and mind. We are the creators of this life as quantum beings. If this feels like a spoiler alert, we apologize. We feel that it's time the world wakes up and we come together to live an extraordinary life on a beautiful Earth of peace and harmony.

"YOU NEED POWER, ONLY WHEN YOU WANT TO DO SOMETHING HARMFUL; OTHERWISE, LOVE IS ENOUGH TO GET EVERYTHING DONE."
-CHARLIE CHAPLIN

Together, we can accomplish much more and have much more fun! We don't have to fight each other for resources, judge each other, fight, bicker, and complain. We can remember that we are all in this together and meant to work together. Let's rid the world of ego and establish world peace. Together, humanity can do anything. Divided, we are only causing unnecessary stress brought upon by greed, corruption, and selfishness. Wake up people; it's time to change the world. How do you want to live your best life? We hope it isn't with greed, corruption, and selfishness. If so, we're sorry to tell you that you will be the outcast, the minority, and the odd one out of the party very soon. Are we done playing this game by the rules of the few who shield us from these truths for their own amusement? It sure seems like we, the people, are fed up with this game. Are we ready to turn the tables, flip the script, and change the tides? We believe that we, the people, are long overdue.

The quality of life is what matters, not the quantity. As far as we know, the quantity of life is one. Even if we live multiple lives, we should make the best of this life; why wouldn't we? If it's less than one for whatever reason and nothing matters, we should still want to make the best of a random, chaotic, and meaningless life. We are all in this together. If not by the collective consciousness, then by the ties of humanity. We should not seek to do anything less than leave this world better than we found. We should aim to increase the quality of life for society and humanity as much as possible. Live this life together, hand in hand, marching forward into the future that humanity at its best brings. We were not born to fight each other. We fight for survival, and we no longer live in survival. We only feel we are fighting to survive when we live in a society that separates each other instead of including each other. When we focus on our differences, we create war; when we focus on our similarities, we create peace. We can make this life a free and beautiful place to live amongst each other in peace. The only thing stopping us is ourselves and those who pit us against each other. When we can get past our ego and lift the veil that those in power have placed over our eyes, it enables us to recognize that we are, in fact, one. With this understanding, we can accomplish world peace and live harmoniously. Put down your swords and open your mind.

We have a dream that one day, the whole world will join together as a world democracy. And that world democracy will find a way to create peace on Earth. We will finally set aside our differences and come together for humanity! Why are we fighting each other? Why are we divided? What is the gain in it all? Power. Destroy the power so that no one may have it. Power only breeds greed, selfishness, and corruption. Many of our current systems are good on paper, but when corrupted with greed, they fail. We don't need to feel greed; we can all share this world, our collective experiences, and our knowledge and grow from it.

Let's all join together to help one another and help humanity thrive. We shouldn't live in survival mode, barely getting by, constantly struggling, constantly worried, blaming each other for everything, separating ourselves into groups only to battle one another. We can stop fighting if we stop seeing each other as the enemy. We are all human, and humans are not our enemy! Do you think we were put on this Earth to fight or help each other? We're pretty sure we all have the same answer for that question regardless of our religious and political beliefs, our gender, our skin color, or our mental health. We, the people, can come together and do amazing things. Why would we stand in the way of that future? Only those who are greedy, power-hungry, and selfish would fight that future as a reality. Dictators free themselves, but they enslave the people. And they won't go down without a fight. Let's hope it's a peaceful one because, after all, they are also human, and at their core, they feel a passion for helping humanity and other humans, even other creatures. We don't have to fight; there doesn't have to be war. War only decides who is left, not who is right. Peace is the answer. We shall come together and figure out what needs to be done to change this world. When we do, we won't need to fight the current system or those who run it. We will create our own system and leave their old systems behind. Together, we will figure out what is best for our human race. And together, we will thrive and live the most beautiful lives in the history of mankind. It's time for world peace. We aim to achieve this by bringing the people together; that is precisely what we will do!

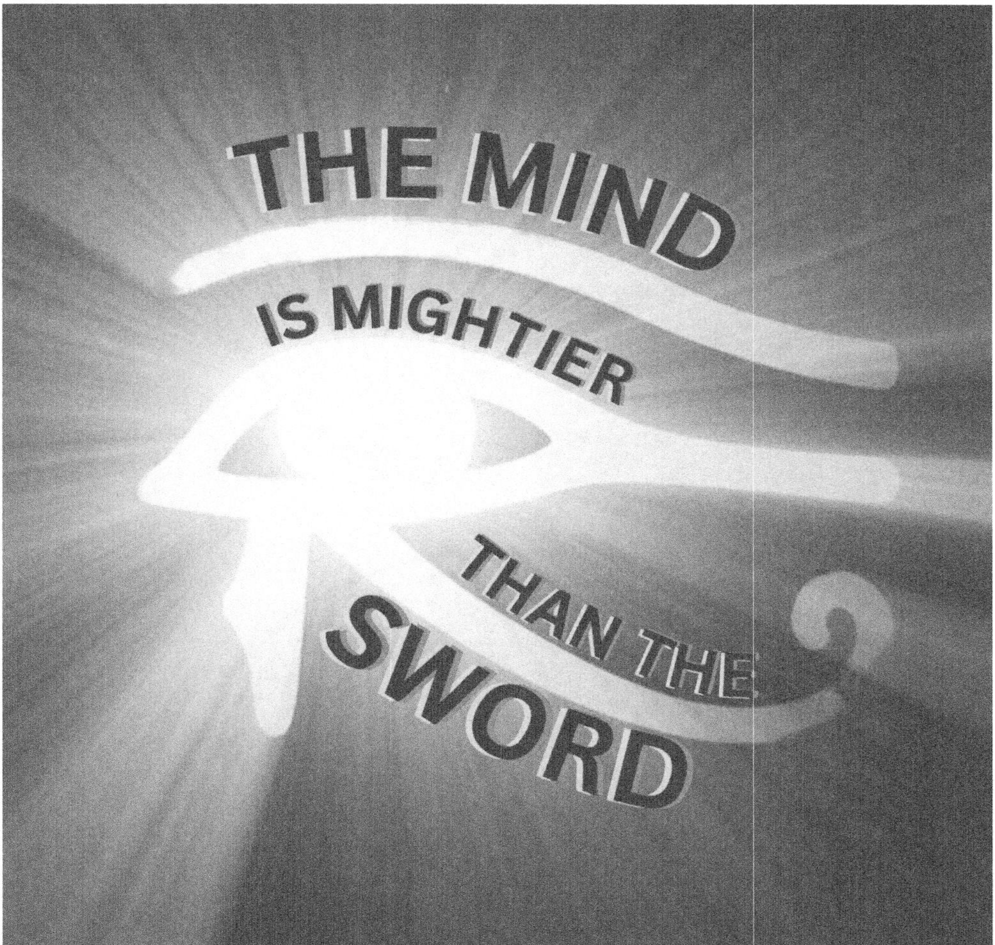
THE MIND
IS MIGHTIER
THAN THE
SWORD

Suppose you want to join our community, watch our YouTube videos, buy our designs, become a teacher of this work, or attend seminars, retreats, or conventions. In that case, you can find us online everywhere. Look for our two logos (the lips and the tree of life/peace symbol) and look for our name: LIVE YOUR BEST LIFE (LYBL) or LYBL Movement. Thank you for taking the time to read our book! Now go out and LIVE YOUR BEST LIFE! Follow us and come together to help us achieve WORLD PEACE!